Praise for

STOP BUYING BINS
& other blunt but practical advice from a home organizer

and

STOP PUSHING PERFECTION
& just create a home you can actually keep neat

"Amazing book about organizing, spoken with both wit and tough love. As a professional organizer myself, many of the stories I can relate to. This book is an easy read and a must for anyone wanting to better manage their clutter!"

"I'm a newbie professional organizer and I've been reading as much as I can about the business. OMG, what a great book! I've read a lot of books and yours, hands down, was my favorite and I never wanted it to end. I appreciate your wit and tough love approach. Can we be best friends?"

"Your book is so well written, and reads like a conversation you would have with an obviously bright friend. I have so many decluttering books, and I'm always hoping I will hit on just the right one that will fix me once and for all. This is it."

"This is a great read! Super enjoyable and an ultimately effective book. The processes are ruthless in the best ways, but not lacking compassion. And I laughed and laughed."

"I would hire her services in a heartbeat. This book is the next best thing."

"I really enjoyed this read. I am currently downsizing for my retirement and it makes me ready to go and sort through more bins to donate, trash, or recycle."

"I just finished this book and will be reading it again, immediately! I found myself laughing, reflecting, getting inspired, and picking my jaw up off the floor! I'm so excited to be implementing her techniques! A must read for anyone with any amount of possessions!"

"I have read SO many books on decluttering, organizing, etc. This is the most fun and motivating book of them all! Everyone has issues and Bonnie gives clear and easy ways to help with yours. If you want long-term solutions that will make your life better forever, read this book!"

"Great easy read book that helps you develop a different mindset. I've read a lot of organizing books. This one is my favorite."

"I just spent the morning reading through your book. Excellent, psychologically wise advice about reframing clients' mindsets about their stuff. I love your common sense advice."

"This is truly an excellent book. I've read several books on organizing, minimizing, decluttering, but this one was really the best one yet. It is because the author talked about the psychological aspects of organizing and decluttering which is very important."

"By far the best ever book for decluttering and staying that way! Loved the way the book is written in stages of decluttering. You actually feel like you are there and she is talking to you! I will read this book again just in case I missed anything and simply for pleasure!"

"This is one of the best books I have read. I appreciate the author's bluntness but there is also a lot of compassion for her clients and readers. Her advice is sound, thorough, and easy to follow. There is a lot of good information in this book. Strongly recommend it."

"This is the book I have needed for years. Twenty some years of storing stuff has now been put on notice now that I have the tools to get rid of so much that is taking up room. This book has given me ways to face boxes of things that have overstayed their welcome and I am ready to start."

"Bonnie Borromeo Tomlinson offers a no-nonsense, humor laden approach to managing your home and belongings."

"She has a great writer's voice. I would certainly like to meet her in person. She's got a great sense of humor!!!"

"Bonnie, the title of your book made me laugh out loud because it's so true! I know a few people who can use this book so I'll be picking up multiple copies."

"Bonnie sets just the right tone, and through her stories she makes you think deeply about your own clutter and desired changes. I've read a lot of books about clutter and decluttering, but Bonnie is the organizer I would hire if I could. I think it would actually be fun to work with her and I believe she would be a friend by the time we were done."

"Love Bonnie's salty style. She's spot on with her observations on the why of overconsumption and the why of breaking the cycle."

"This was the most helpful book I've read about downsizing (and I've read many). It was well-written. Several times I laughed out loud: 'Bins give you the impression that you are organized when all you've actually done is box your garbage.' I look forward to more books by this author!"

"I've read at least a half dozen books about home organization. Stop Buying Bins is my favorite. I was inspired to begin purging within minutes of reading this. Thank you, Bonnie, if you publish another book, perhaps on decorating, I'll buy that one, too."

"If you do not know where to start, this book is step one."

"The second book in the Stop Buying Bins series is even better than the first."

"Bonnie Borromeo Tomlinson has done it again with "Stop Pushing Perfection". This is another great book to help get you organized! My book just arrived and I started reading it immediately! Now I just need to put her advice into action!"

Also by Bonnie Borromeo Tomlinson:

STOP BUYING BINS
& other blunt but practical advice
from a home organizer

STOP PUSHING PERFECTION
& just create a home you
can actually keep neat

YOU DON'T NEED IT

& other motherly advice from a home organizer on setting up your first home

Bonnie Borromeo Tomlinson

Yellow Lab Press
AMHERST, MASS

Copyright Disclaimer:
The information and advice contained in this book are based upon the personal and professional experiences of the author. The publisher and author are not responsible for any consequences resulting from the use of any of the suggestions, preparations, or procedures discussed in this book. Names and identifying details have been changed and fictionalized to protect the privacy of any individuals. In all cases, the retelling of any personal events are composites of multiple projects worked on by the author.

Copyright © 2025 by Bonnie Borromeo Tomlinson

All rights reserved. No part of this book may be reproduced or transmitted in any form or by any means, electronic or mechanical, including photocopying, recording, or by any information or retrieval systems, without the permission of the publisher.

Printed in the United States of America.

Editor: David W. Edelstein
Proofreader: Gillian Tomlinson
Book and cover design: David W. Edelstein
Author photograph by: Yellow Lab Press

Yellow Lab Press
Amherst, MA 01002

ISBN: 978-1-7378818-4-1 (paperback)
ISBN: 978-1-7378818-5-8 (ebook)

Subjects:
Nonfiction | How-To | House and Home | Self-Help | Decorating | Organizing | Cleaning
HOM019000

For My Daughter's Remarkable Group of Friends
at Mount Holyoke College
in the Class of 2025 who assisted me throughout
the writing of this book.

And for Gilly...*Always*

Acknowledgments

I have been lucky enough to have lifelong friendships. Some I speak with nearly every day. Others I haven't spoken to in years, but the moment we reach out, it's like no time has passed. Each and every one of them has kept me afloat on this journey of life through its many ebbs and flows. They are not fair-weather friends. They remind me that above all else, my back is covered, they're in my corner, and I am loved. I am the person I am growing into because of them and I could not be more grateful. There are too many to name. Just know, my friends, I value what we have together beyond measure. And that love and support is a two-way street. I've always got your back, I'm always in your corner, and I love you.

* * *

To Jane Nikander and Rebecca Brown of Wilton Public & Gregg Free Library in Wilton, NH: You persuaded me to speak at your beautiful library, and this opened a whole new world. I hadn't even considered doing speaking engagements and now my calendar is full. I can't thank you both enough for the encouragement, new friendships, and most of all, common humor and mindset. I'm jealous you two got to work with each other every day. Though I have a feeling the three of us together would get very little work done. *Haha.* Thank you both beyond measure.

* * *

To David (of David W. Edelstein Text & Design) in Nova Scotia, Canada: I am thrilled to be working on our third book together! Your skills as a book designer are impeccable. But your ability to translate my ideas into cover art is what makes this collaboration really work. Thank you for your prompt responses to my somewhat endless revisions: "Can you shift the text a little up and to the right and maybe make the red a bit deeper?" I quite literally could not have done this without you. Especially now that you have also taken on the duties of editor! Thank you! Thank you!

* * *

What would my acknowledgments be without thanking my daughter Gillian "Gilly" Tomlinson. I wake up each morning saying two things to myself *(maybe three if my knees hurt.)* One, do something today your future self will thank you for. And two, get up and create a legacy your daughter can be proud of. Every day you make me proud to be your mother, and it drives me forward to create and do good work. I love you "chick".

A Note from the Author

I was in my local library standing in the stacks—the 700's in Dewey decimal to be exact, as is my comfort zone. Next to me were two young women from UMass Amherst. They were perusing interior design books looking for inspiration to decorate their off-campus apartment.

"Whoa, this one is gorgeous! What do you think?"

"We can't afford that book, much less the furniture in that picture."

"Sure we can. We just need to win the lottery." They laughed, closed the book, and put it back on the shelf. "Let's go get boba."

It occurred to me at that moment that there is a real need for a book designed for those just starting their lives beyond their parents' home or a college dorm room. One that would show them money doesn't buy style, and any look can be achieved on a shoestring. One that would put them on a path of less clutter, fewer poor purchases, and more 'life' in their living situations. One with the advice I'd like to impart to my own daughter, who is on the last lap of her college career and will soon be living on her own. A quick Google search showed there were only a handful of books with only a faint commonality, and the subject of my next book was decided.

* * *

I have made a lot of house and home mistakes in my 50+ years, from purchasing the "right" things, to overstocking "essentials," to decorating "on trend." Now, after years in the home organizing and decorating business, working in my own homes as well as those of my clients, I've gained a wealth of knowledge while also straightening out my priorities. And I'd like to gift what I've learned to the next generation of home-nesters.

My hope is that the ideas presented in the following pages will save you time and money, rescue castoff items while also reducing waste in our landfills, and put in motion habits that will benefit your lifelong organized lifestyle and financial future.

You may be asking, "is that even possible?" It's not only possible, it's rewarding. And your home will be a true reflection of you in the process. I promise.

Contents

Introduction... 1

PART 1: BEFORE & DURING YOUR MOVE

1. Imagining a Home of YOUR Dreams................ 7

2. Measure. Plan. Scrub............................. 25

3. Find Free Before Financing....................... 49

PART 2: THE FIRST SIX MONTHS

4. Keep Organizing In Mind........................ 79

5. Learn How To Live In Your Space 101

6. Decorate With Restraint 135

PART 3: FOREVER AFTER

7. "Use It Up, Wear It Out, Make It Do,
   or Do Without".................................. 153

8. Pretend You Have to Flee 169

9. Don't Live in Lack 177

Final Advice 201

Introduction

Welcome to your first home on your own!

Maybe you are living alone in an apartment, or in a house with a group of friends. Or the other way around. In any scenario, you are beginning the process of setting up house. You are no doubt considering what you need and what you want and what you can fit and what you can afford. You are excited and YOU SHOULD BE! Soak in every moment. But also slow down and take a beat. I'm going to try to help you stave off A LOT of firstie mistakes, *AND help the world in the process,* so please hear me out.

It has become written into our cultural DNA that more = better. But retail therapy and "keeping up with the Joneses" has led to generations of accumulated objects that have not only resulted in clutter and debt, but also a deeper sense of lack. On top of which, the desire for new and improved, bigger and better, has birthed a mindset of obsolescence where making due with what one has, or repairing what's broken, are concepts rarely even considered. We waste more money than we make, we have more possessions than we actually use, and the landfills have reached maximum capacity in the process.

Sadly, you are entering a shaky adulthood plagued by financial instability, global climate change, social inequality, and a 24-hour, in-real-time news cycle that puts it all front and center. I won't for a second suggest this book has the solutions to any of those issues, but what it will provide are some alternatives when it comes to setting up and outfitting your homes. Ones that will save you money, help you avoid contributing to fast furnishings, and might just make you happier, which will in turn make the world a better place to live. *Tall order for a book about organizing and decorating, but let's give it a shot, shall we?*

I'm not suggesting a life barren of trinkets or even opulence. Just one where a bit of care and attention to how you "keep house" can make a world of difference. Ultimately, you'll be creating less work, more time, deeper joy, greater financial savings, less stress, and an overall sense of well-being. *Whew.* If it sounds too good to be true, I'll attempt to prove it all in the following pages. Along the way there will be **decorating tips, organizing systems, cleaning habits, hands-on upcycling projects, and even some estimated costs.** *Let's see if we can stretch the budget as far as possible.*

My hope is that this book will be a roadmap for a new generation of home nesters who are willing to step out of the conventional guidelines of

"what one MUST own" and think economically and responsibly while also tapping into their individual happiness. The generations that have come before are leaving you quite a mess in more ways than one. My goal is to do what can be done to help you escape the burden of more. *Surprisingly enough, you might really enjoy yourself along the way.*

Part 1

BEFORE & DURING YOUR MOVE

1

Imagining a Home of YOUR Dreams

There is a lengthy list of advice I would impart to those feathering a first nest beyond a dorm room or a bedroom at home. That list doesn't include the prerequisite things one might somehow feel obligated to purchase. It doesn't include a harrowing trip to IKEA and a U-Haul filled with flat-pack furniture and a set of Allen wrenches. It most certainly does not include filling up on mass-produced organizers that only serve supposed purposes—*sock organizers, really?* No, the first thing on the list would be to ponder, think, and muse before acquiring a single shower curtain.

So, where to start? I'll tell you where **not** to start. Any big box store for any set of things. "Oh, look at this rotating caddy filled with kitchen utensils? That's perfect." *Is it though?* For one, look at the size of that thing. That's going to take up a ton of counter space. Plus it's plastic, so how long before it starts getting grungy and you wind up tossing it? And the utensils...*do you even know what half of them are for?* Are they useful, or better put, will you ever use them? Now that perfect rotating plastic kitchen caddy filled with utensils you can't name doesn't look as good as you thought, does it? *Okay, let's move on.*

Bed-in-a-bag? *Please don't.* Layers of window treatments? *Say no.* Box set of four place settings of dinner plate, bowl, cup, and saucer? *When have you ever used a saucer?* Look, you're not required to follow some packing list sent home before summer camp. I'm letting you off the hook here and now...**you are not required to have anything in your home that you don't want, that holds no meaning, that you won't use, or that is disposable or short-term, just because someone else deemed it "essential."**

My point is this. Simply put, you are just beginning to accumulate household objects. Before you dive headlong into buying things, **consider your space, your needs, and your lifestyle.** Yes, you will likely need a table to eat or work at...*unless you do neither of those things at a table. See what I mean?* **You don't need it unless YOU need it.**

* * *

This is the first thing I'd like you to do:
Go to the grocery store or drug store or wherever

magazines are still sold and pick up a bunch of home decor magazines that catch your eye. Maybe even some that don't; you never know where inspiration will strike. Likewise, follow decor magazines on Instagram and Pinterest.

TOTAL COST: $4.95 (cover price) - $29.95 (special edition) each

Start amassing a collection of pictures you are drawn to. **Don't pigeonhole yourself into thinking your tastes lie in a certain style or period or even color, by convincing yourself that's who you are.** And even if you know what you like, know here and now your tastes will evolve. So in this moment, just collect pictures of interiors that make you stop and consider them. Don't seek them out either; they will find you. They don't all have to tell the same story because oddly enough, together, they will tell the true story of what makes you happy. I'll say it again, don't push for one idea. You may love Japanese manga, but that doesn't mean you must therefore also love shoji screens and tatami mats. Let it flow.

Collect all these pictures and make a vision board, either virtually or on a cork board. I'm old school when it comes to an inspiration board, so I like the tactile nature of photos and tacks I can move around. There is something visually stunning about seeing interiors you are drawn to, all in one place. It is art. *In fact, there you go, your first piece of wall decor.*

PROJECT: VISION BOARD
- bulletin board (as large as your space and cash will allow)
- fabric large enough to cover it
- fabric ribbon *optional*
- tacks

I've done this project myself several times for various situations. Since you will be covering the board, it's a perfect opportunity to use something secondhand that may already be marked up. The last time I wanted to make one, I sent an email out to my neighborhood asking if anyone had a cork board they weren't using that I could buy from them. Two people wrote back; both gave me them for free.

Choose a piece of fabric large enough to wrap the board on all sides and staple it to the back. I suggest a textured material like upholstery fabric. Using a tight woven fabric like twill will show all the tack holes.

Poke tacks into the board so they are readily available when you want to hang something. You can use thumb tacks (flat, usually metal), push pins (come in various colors, plastic or metal), or even upholstery tacks (like thumb tacks but more ornate).

You could also use ribbon in a crisscross pattern across the face of the board, and like the fabric, staple it to the back. Tack down where the ribbons intersect each other and then tuck photos or notes behind the ribbon instead of using tacks.

TOTAL COST: FREE - $30

With your inspiration board in front of you, a commonality in those photos will emerge. Are you drawn to a particular color palette? Do you prefer the minimalist lines of Scandinavian design or something more cottagecore maximalist? Dark wood furniture versus floral, overstuffed, upholstered pieces? Mid-century Modern or Art Nouveau? Or maybe you love it all and you gravitate towards a look that is truly eclectic? You are beginning to curate your own aesthetic…and it's all good. There is no right or wrong here, just you.

Before I moved to the house I currently live in, I downsized from a much larger house. As time-consuming as it was to find ways to purge so many items, it was also really exciting, paring back to just what I wanted in my new home, in my new life. And I could **shop from my own stock** and pick and choose just the items that worked. How did I decide what was moving with me? I made a vision board based on my space, my needs, and my new lifestyle. **Back then, thinking ahead, I only had three things to consider:**

SPACE: My post-and-beam home is a nod to Japanese interiors and American mid-century architecture—and gives me a treehouse vibe.

NEEDS: I would be writing, sleeping, cooking, and doing the usual household chores. But rarely entertaining large groups to a sit down meal or hosting parties.

LIFESTYLE: I would be living alone, except when my daughter was home from college, so most of the time it only has to work for me.

After that, everything fell into place. You likely won't be burdened with downsizing before accumulating for your first move, but the same principles apply—**your space, your needs, your lifestyle.** Now, look at your vision board and start making real choices.

I'll give you an example. Imagine everything on your vision board gives off a cozy feel. It is filled with photos of quilts and plants and books and a cat curled up on a window ledge. Equal parts English cottage and Danish Hygge (pronounced Hoo-gah), with a dash of great grandma. That then is the look that most speaks to what you want your home to feel like. Now consider your space. It seems like a no-brainer that a reading nook will be in the plans—next to the window where there are built-in bookshelves. If there are no bookshelves or a bookcase, **add them to your acquisition list. Notice I didn't say "shopping list." We'll discuss that more later.** You also don't have a big comfy chair and footrest. And the floor lamp from your dorm room, which was cool when you bought it, is just not going to work for you now. As for the extras, you've got the books, *which no doubt you'll add to,* and plants your friends have all agreed to gift you as apartment-warming gifts, but you don't have any quilts or a cat. Your list would read:

- Bookshelves or bookcase (confirm with your landlord that you can hang heavy-duty brackets if you're going with shelves)
- Comfy armchair, as oversized as the space will permit
- Coordinating footrest or ottoman
- Mismatched but coordinating (for the look) warm and cozy quilts
- Possibly a cat (confirm with your landlord you can have pets)

It's really that simple. **Start with the space you envision first and grow from there.** In fact, once you have your nook carved out, that may be enough decorating for the moment. There is no rush to fill it all up. The concept of "more" is a slippery slope to clutter, while open space can be a surprisingly freeing blessing.

You Don't Need It

* * *

Now it's time for a monkey wrench or two. **If you are living alone, your only compromises will come in the form of what you can fit and what you can afford. But if you are living with a group of friends or a partner, you will have to cull together your tastes and find a commonality you are all willing to embrace.** At least for the common spaces. Believe it or not, they can be found in the unlikeliest of combos. Take the examples listed below:

> Example 1: Minimalist Scandi design and maximalist cottagecore both favor light colors, organic fabrics, airy spaces, natural light, and the outdoors inside with plants and flowers.

> Example 2: Dark wood furniture and floral overstuffed upholstered pieces are not mutually exclusive. You can easily pair dark furnishings with light-colored table linens and floral fabric decor accessories; the combos are infinite thereafter.

> Example 3: Let's do mid-century and Art Nouveau. That one seems more difficult, but both styles make wood the star and use organic shapes, so at their core they are really very similar.

SIDE STORY: In my dreams, owning an Eames lounger and ottoman (mid-century) paired with a

Tiffany wisteria lamp (Art Nouveau) would be an all-time amazing duo. And while someone who is paying down student loan debts is probably not in the market for any of those pieces, secondhand reproductions are out there if you are up to the challenge of searching.

TOTAL COST: $2K (new reproduction) – $530K (vintage authentic)

OK. Let's get back to reality here. My point is that connections can be made between very opposing tastes. **What is probably more important when you are sharing space with others is how you will cohabitate, and in this case, an individual's design inclination can be an indication of their lifestyle habits.**

Does one housemate's minimalistic tastes clash with another's budding collections? Are organization and cleanliness important to all? How does everyone plan to keep the place clean and organized? These questions are as important as smoker versus non-smoker, or cat owner versus allergic to cats. You've decided to make a go of this living situation together, so before nails are hammered into walls and paintings are hung, come to those mutual understandings before things go south. Compromises will have to be made. When it comes to style, there is very little you CAN'T make work together. What is more difficult to coordinate is how you live. That will drive how you decorate.

Let's put this in practical terms. Let's say you and

your best friend are moving in together. You've each created your own inspiration board for your dream home. They are not exactly the same, but close enough, as they are both giving off a very modern, streamlined vibe. The problem comes when you begin to discuss common space. You'd like it minimal with light-colored natural woods that tend to hide dust, because you know cleaning is not your cup of tea. She'd like glass and chrome, plus a place, preferably by a window, for her easel and paints—the same window you were hoping to put that reproduction Eames lounger and ottoman your parents are letting you take from their house. How do you make this work? Talk it out. How you navigate these situations will give you some insight into how blending your styles (both furniture and living) will ultimately work.

- It's not worth losing your best friend over any of this, so **treat it less like a negotiation and more like a mutually beneficial project.**
- **Discuss needs first.** She needs the natural light to paint. You need to find room for the lounger and ottoman. It makes more sense for her to have the window, for which she agrees to keep her supplies neat and in closed storage. She also agrees to purchase you a floor lamp to use with your lounger so you can set it somewhere else in the room.

- Neither of you has any other furniture at the moment, so it's a perfect time to **discuss maintenance.** Glass and chrome require constant cleaning due to fingerprints and dust. Your roommate says she will handle it; you know in your heart, she won't. Gently suggest the glass and chrome pieces be limited to accessories instead of furnishings. That way they can be hand washed in the sink as needed instead of having to be cleaned constantly.

- Now, **what do you each want this space to be for?** Netflix and relaxing = big sofa and large TV. Weekly board game/wine tasting friend night = long dining table and multiple chairs. Individual hobby spaces = her paints and your reading area, which means no more furniture needed. Discuss the big picture and plot your wants accordingly.

- **Discuss finances. Or in other words, who pays for what?** My suggestion would be to each acquire pieces individually. That way, when one day you separate assets, you can each leave with your own items. But maybe you can't fund it alone. Discuss a budget that works for you both and come to an agreement on how property will be divided in the future. Right now you may be all about sharing, but down the road, who knows? For your own peace of mind, make a plan for the possibility of a less cordial future.

- **How will you acquire all the things you have determined you will need, and how will you pay for them?** There are several avenues. Buying from a brick-and-mortar store or online is easy enough, but not nearly as fun and certainly more expensive than hunting and gathering. Might I suggest a few more options: antique stores, vintage stores, secondhand stores, thrift stores, yard sales, family, friends, and strangers via Buy Nothing. The world is filled with retail, resale, or free opportunities.

* * *

There is one last piece to the puzzle. No matter your living arrangements, now is an ideal time to cultivate your design principles and philosophies.

WARNING: Things are going to get a bid judgmental here, but reserve your response until you've read further and have all the facts. I ask of you the following questions:

- Is how you live important to you? *(I assume it is since you're reading this book. If it is not, please only live with someone of like mind. For someone who cares about their surroundings and how they are kept, living with someone who doesn't is a recipe for constant aggravation.)*

- Is buying new and/or designer pieces important to you? *(Budgeting for such an expense must be considered and may not be everyone's priority. Also, care and upkeep to maintain these pieces are part of the cost.)*

- Is buying secondhand furnishings, whether antique, vintage, thrifted, or giveaway, a nonstarter subject? *(Consider that this option provides less expensive and often higher quality choices. Previously owned does not equal trash.)*

- Are you opposed to refurbishing or upcycling older pieces and decor? *(You may think you don't have the time, space, or skill set, but YouTube tutorials would suggest otherwise. I'm not saying to go out and rent a bandsaw. I'm saying most of what is available in the secondhand marketplace just needs to be cleaned.)*

- Do you think purchasing all-pressboard, build-it-yourself furniture is a cheap and cheerful way to furnish your entire home? *(It has its benefits to be sure, but bear in mind that "fast furniture" manufacturing contributes to the pollution of our planet and the abundance of castoffs in landfills.)*

- Do you think it's important to take care of your things so they last? *(If not, treating your things as only "good enough until you have better" breeds a mindset of lack. We'll discuss this one in more detail later in the book.)*

- Do you think it's important to have all the "right" things as a matter of pride? *(If your income allows for it, who am I to question it? But if money is tight, put things in perspective and prioritize. Saving to buy is always a better financial option than credit, even if it does delay immediate gratification.)*

In the following chapters we will discuss these in more depth. **For now, find your style, determine how you'd like to live, and set your priorities in motion. Even though you are just starting out, what you do today could very well make the difference in your future.** That is not to say any mistakes or errors in judgment will result in irreparable harm—*we are only talking about interior decorating here after all.* But let me give you an example of what I mean with a little game of Would You Rather.

Would you rather autopay $100 a month for the next seven years to some discount furniture store that likely will go out of business before you have paid off the principal on that complete dining room set that doesn't actually fit in your apartment now? OR would you rather pay $100 for a table and six chairs at Goodwill, take it home, and wash and paint it to coordinate with your tastes, and then likely keep it forever, downgrading it to a kids' craft table at some point down the road?

TOTAL COST: $8,400 (and you hate it after a few years because the veneer is peeling off the pressboard) vs. $150 (with paint/supplies.)

That's a difference of $8,250! Money like that could go to so many more important expenses, it's mind-blowing. I get it. You're in your 20s, you've got time to make more money, and you think $100 a month is something you can easily cover, so why not? "Why not?" looks a lot like two weeks in Europe—*and that's nice hotels and cabs, not youth hostels and the Metro.*

The point of all of this is to say:

- New is not better and used is not garbage because not only are secondhand furnishings relatively cheap, they are often better made than mass-produced products.

- Mass-produced products, or "fast-furniture," are a major contributor of pollutants.

- Reclaiming castoffs and refurbishing them avoids adding to landfills. Plus learning new skills in order to upcycle old, unloved items is empowering and just plain fun.

- Curating your knick knacks (bric-a-brac, stuff, crap, whatever you want to call it) will result in less clutter, which equals less cleaning and organizing and downsizing later.

- Caring for your possessions cultivates gratitude. Treating your possessions like garbage is a reflection of your self-worth. *This is a biggie.*

I think that's enough for now. **To recap:**

1. **Slow down and think first.**
2. **Determine your style.**
3. **Discuss connections and compromises with those you are living with.**
4. **Form your acquisition philosophy.**

Once you've got all that in order, it's time to move onto the nuts and bolts and electric drills of it all. It may seem easier to just head to Target and buy the upgraded version of your dorm room essentials, but it's not. It's just not. I will explain the hows and whys in more detail. For now, be inspired, be creative, be excited. You are taking a major life step. Work gloves suggested.

TOTAL COST: $7 - $18
(depending on brand and material)

* * *

STORY TIME FROM BEFORE YOUR TIME

Dreaming in the days before my first apartment, I wanted so badly to come home at the end of every work day to the Georgetown townhouse owned by Murphy Brown. Many if not all of you born in the 21st century have never seen the sitcom "Murphy Brown" that ran for 10 seasons on CBS. Inspired by that character, portrayed brilliantly by Candice Bergen, I often found myself hoping the scenes would wind up in her home instead of the newsroom. Elegant yet comfortable. Grand yet homey. Like an heirloom cashmere cardigan. Quality that stands the test of time, well loved and enjoyed.

As you consider all the details of your new home, consider too how you want it to feel and how you want to feel in it. There is no right or wrong answer. Only what is yours.

2

Measure. Plan. Scrub.

I am beyond excited for you as you venture out on your own...*and maybe just a teeny bit jealous.* **You never get a second chance to experience your first home for the first time.** I can still remember opening the front door to my very own apartment. A mix of excitement and pride and independence and anxiety. All blended with a rush of adrenaline and motivation to make it my own as soon as possible—and thus began all the usual newbie nesting mistakes.

I've been thinking a lot about that apartment, and not just because I'm writing this book for you, the first-time home nester. But because as I sit here solidly in midlife reflection, pondering the roads we take, I'm wishing I had had someone to tell me the things I'm about to tell you. Not just how to set up a living situation, but about journeys and where they take us. About being true to yourself. About being more aware of how and where you spend your money, time, and attention. About taking paths that might not be considered usual but will still get you to a successful life—a life you are grateful to wake up to each day. So if you'll indulge me, let me regale you with my story.

* * *

It was roughly 18 months after my college graduation. I had saved enough money between my 9-5 job in advertising and my part-time gig working at the Gap nights and weekends to finally move out on my own alone. I found a third story walk-up in a row house on a quiet street in Hoboken, which for those of you unfamiliar, is a city in New Jersey across the Hudson River from Manhattan. My hours-long commute by bus or train from either of my parents' homes into NYC was now just 20 minutes. And it cost $1.25 each way instead of the $100 plus for a monthly pass from the suburbs. *Those are early '90s prices, by the way, God only knows what it costs now.* Of course, any extra money saved on commuting was immediately filtered to rent and utilities, so my bank account was always in catch-up mode. But I was living on my own and it was all worth it.

In my haste to start living my single-girl life in the city, I jumped headlong into a bunch of classic mistakes. From bringing too much furniture from home without first measuring the space, to buying build-it-yourself storage without taking into account the weight of the boxes or how to get them up the stairs, I was in the thick of making and correcting mistakes, wasting money I didn't have, growing credit card debt, and ultimately feeling pretty stupid. Here are the mistakes I made that should be avoided:

- **Not measuring first.** Having only ever eyeballed the space during my initial walkthrough, I moved my entire childhood bedroom suite (twin bed with headboard and footboard plus mattress and box spring, long dresser with mirror, a chest of drawers, and a standing mirror) from Boonton Township, NJ, to Hoboken, without first considering whether it would all fit. With the help of friends and their caravan of cars and minivans, *and the incentive of pizza and beer,* they helped me move it all up and in. Now, one could say that that was the responsible thing to do—no new furniture purchases, friends helping with the move. What I haven't mentioned is that while the apartment was classified as a one bedroom, there was no other living space besides the oddly huge kitchen and the disproportionately large bathroom. Which meant all this furniture was going to be in one room. "Well, wasn't it all in one room in the first place?" you ask. Oh but wait, let me continue.

- **Bringing more than I needed.** In addition to the bedroom furniture, my mother had given me a large, heavy shag rug, a Victorian loveseat, and a steamer trunk. An odd assortment to be sure, but beggars can't be choosers, and I did in fact need a rug, a couch, and a TV stand respectively. Somehow I managed to stuff it all in there. Even still, that's a lot to ask of a single room. You could call the design aesthetic "unnecessarily overcrowded eclectic." And that's all before any decoration dressing.

- My next mistake was **declining a fresh coat of paint from my landlord and saying I would do it myself.** I was so excited to move in, I told my new landlord (who lived on the first two floors of the house) I would paint once I moved in if he just provided the supplies. *What the actual hell was I thinking!?* I'm not a painter. I had never painted before. Add to the mix that I'm five feet tall and the room had 10' ceilings (drop ceilings, thankfully, or it would have been even taller) and I did not own a ladder. Let's just wrap up this one by saying, I started painting behind the door to test my skills and that's as far as I got.

- **Not investing in a folding stepladder, even if you're tall.** I'm short. Stuff is high. The chances of me growing taller were slim to none, so it was a safe bet I should have invested in a sturdy multi-step stepladder back then. *I will always need a step ladder; I currently own three.* Had I owned one back then, I could have made a better start with the painting. Or at least taken advantage of the cabinets above the closet doors. *Who knows what was up there the whole time I lived in that apartment?*

TOTAL COST: $25 - $90 (price varies based on height, weight, folding function)

- **Buying furniture without considering the logistics.** Somehow, even though I was bursting at the seams furniture-wise, I decided in my infinite wisdom I could use a small desk and some storage units to take advantage of the extra space in the kitchen. I'm going to skip to the end of this tale and give you the lesson. You should never go shopping at IKEA alone, buy flat-pack furniture, roll it out to your vehicle, have to go back into the store to get an attendant to help put it in the car, drive home, double park on a crowded city street, and THEN realize, "how the Hell am I going to get this upstairs?" all while having people lay on their car horns because you're blocking the road.

SIDE STORY: Back then I used the desk to start writing my first novel. *I never finished it, and upon rereading* *it recently I've determined it is not worth the paper it's typed on.*

- **Buying new when there is plenty of old.** I hadn't yet leaned into my true nature of salvaging second-hand. If I had, I would have outfitted my kitchen with castoffs from my parents' homes. Or at least bought what I needed from a local Salvation Army. Instead, I bought new, cheap (quality, not price) dishes, pots, pans, utensils, knives, silverware, glasses, etc., etc. from a department store. Think kitchen-in-a-box. All of which eventually fell apart, or I broke, or I did not clean properly and had to throw away. It was a complete waste of money. Even more so because I didn't need most of it in the first place, since I ate close to all of my meals out.

- **Decorating with meaningless mass-produced decor.** "But everyone is doing it. How will I know it's the right thing to own if there aren't 300,000 other people that own it?" Ah, the allure of trendy crap when I didn't have the self-confidence to follow my own path. Who could have known that some American discount store's overstock of Chinese-manufactured tchotchkes would lead me wrong? *Ask me if I still have any of that garbage in my home now. The answer is no.*

- **Last but certainly not least, spending money I didn't have.** As humiliating as this is to admit, I think it's important to note. Having collection agents call you saying they have not received your monthly minimum balance is not the message you want to hear after working two jobs and getting home at midnight on a random Tuesday. Talk about a cautionary tale—I literally decorated my way into credit card debt. There are so many far better ways to personalize your space, and several of them are FREE. I will discuss spending, or rather limiting spending, further along in the book. For now, I think you can surmise where I'm going with this. The moral of that story is: don't open credit cards.

* * *

At the start of the last chapter I advised you to "slow down and think first." By now, you've created your vision board, and you've come to an understanding with your roommates about how you would like it to look as well as how you plan to live together harmoniously. And, just as important, you have given some thought to your philosophies on all future acquisitions, taking into account your feelings on environmental and financial issues. Now it's time to get to work by measuring, planning, and scrubbing.

You Don't Need It

* * *

The rental market moves fast. Like…

"I'd like to see the apartment listed in today's paper."
"Sorry it's already gone."

…fast.

There are likely to be a ton of other applicants looking in the same general area, in the same general price range. You will probably not have the opportunity to leisurely peruse listings while uttering the words "let me think about it," because in the period of mere moments, that place will be gone. In some cases, you may not have the chance to see the space in person before signing a lease, relying instead on photos and descriptions and the word of your rental agent (which in any major city you absolutely need.) **If, however, you do get to see it and have time to take it all in, I suggest you follow this checklist:**

1. **Measure your gut.** The gut knows. First impressions are important. Take in the vibe the neighborhood gives you. Will you live alone, work late, and want to go right to sleep once you're home? Then you need safe surroundings, well-lit streets, and a quiet neighbor. Do you and your roommates love

to party? Then the quiet neighbors probably aren't going to be too happy with you.

2. **Measure your emotions.** As you enter the door, take it all in as if this will be your home. Adjust your expectations against what you can and can't live without. Do you feel happy? Do you feel secure? Are you completely turned off by the filthy carpet in the lobby or intoxicated by the aroma from the bakery next door? Would you be proud to invite your friends over? What about your parents?

   As you measure these internal metrics, consider this. **These are things you should never compromise on, no matter how much you want to live on your own:**

   → **Safety:** I was unwavering in my desire to live in Hoboken—a city famous not only as the birthplace of Frank Sinatra, but also as the square mile with the most bars per capita in the US. As a result, alcohol-related issues are a given. If the over-served aren't singing in the street, they are trying (and sometimes succeeding) to break into cars thinking it's their own. I moved there knowing this from the get-go.
   Lesson: If where you're looking has something you can't put up with, it's time to move on to another zip code.

- **Maintenance:** I wanted to live in a brownstone with a front stoop with ornate iron handrails and maybe a historic marker on the facade. What I found was a brick row house painted blue with basic aluminum handrails and a door in need of some varnish. But it was clean and it was well kept and the landlord was easy to reach if I needed anything. All I had to do was stick a note on his door downstairs.
Lesson: Expect where you're looking to fall below your expectations and know what you're willing to accept.

- **Cost vs value:** At the time, I saw only two apartments. The one I eventually moved into on Park Ave, and another which was larger, only $40 more a month, in a fourth floor walkup on Sixth St. Why did I not go for the bigger one? One, I didn't need more room. Two, forty dollars a month is $480 in a year. Three, avenues are longer than streets and when you're trying to find parking on a Sunday night when everyone is coming back from their weekends out of town, that matters. Lastly, four floors of stairs past three other tenants and no landlord on sight didn't sit well with me.
Lesson: Bigger isn't better if you consider the factors that mean more to you personally.

Measure. Plan. Scrub.

3. **Measure the space.** Finally, we're getting to the literal meaning of the word. Remember to bring a retractable tape measure with you when you look at places. If you don't have one, it's a good investment.

   TOTAL COST: $10 - $30.
   You'll want metal, not plastic or fabric, because the rigidity of metal across large areas is important. And look for one that's around 25' long. You'll have it forever. Tip: there will be a number on the measuring block, 2.5"-3". That's the size of the block itself, so don't forget to add that to your measurement.

   What to measure:

   → **The size of the room,** or what's called the footprint. Measure the width of each wall. If you multiply the measurement of two walls that meet at a corner, you will have the square footage of the room.

   → **The height of the walls, as well as the size of all windows, closets, or any other nooks that take up wall space.** This is important to note for a few reasons including determining how much paint or wallpaper you need, the amount of fabric for window treatments, space for wall art, and where furniture can be placed in a room to not block any of these things.

- **The height and width of doorways.** I had a colleague in those early days who was quite tall. Both he and his wife were imposing figures. They had a custom couch made for their Upper East Side townhouse built specifically for their frames, only to learn upon delivery that it was too big to get through the front door. It had to be taken apart and rebuilt inside. Save yourself the burden (and price tag) and measure the doorways.

4. **Along the same lines as measuring is photographing the space.** Take copious amounts of photos. There are things your eyes will miss that the camera won't.

    - Photograph the front of the building and up and down the street. Not video. Just like your eyes, videos miss details that still photographs pick up.
    - Photograph from the doorway of each room. Taking three to four photos left to right from the doorway should give you an overall look at the entire room.
    - Photograph up and down hallways and staircases.
    - Photograph inside all closets and cabinets.

Why do this? Because you're going to plan ahead. You're not going to hope a piece of furniture works. You're going to know it will. You're going to know that the queen-sized sleeper sofa you want for when friends stay over will fit up the stairs, around the strangely placed pillar which hides plumbing, through the doorway into the room, and that you can place it with enough space to open it into a bed.

A few more things:

- What is the flooring made of? Carpet? Then no need for rugs. Ceramic tile? Then not only do you need rugs but also non-slip padding underneath.

- What are the walls made of? Drywall, plaster, brick? Know the best ways to hang wall decor depending on your wall material, if in fact your landlord permits it at all.

- No dishwasher? You need a drying rack or mat.

- No in-unit washer/dryer? What are the laundry facilities, if the building has them? Or, where is the nearest laundromat?

- Likewise, where is the nearest grocery store, drug store, hospital, police station, fire house, or anything else important to your daily life?

I could go on, but I think your head is sufficiently spinning already. The takeaway is this: Ask yourself if you want to live here even after seeing (and feeling) the space, *and* if your answer is yes, now is the time to arm yourself with all possible information so you can truly make it your own once you get there.

PLAN

It's my absolute favorite step—planning time! Ready? Good. Get out a pen and paper and let's go. You, or you plus any roommate(s), need to sit down and ask yourselves the following:

- **What do you need?** Needs are few and not to be confused with wants. Needs are a bed, a table and chair, a dresser *(unless you hang all your clothes; see how specific a need is?)*

- **What do you have?** That's anything you own yourself, or anything being given to you by your parents, your extended family, or the elderly neighbor down the street who said "take whatever you want" from her garage when you volunteered to clean it out.

- **Who's bringing what?** Don't double up. You don't need two coffee makers. Decide who is bringing what based on which better serves your collective needs.

- **What would you like to acquire?** *Now we're getting into the details.* Make that list of all the things you do not have but would like. Do you personally want a nightstand? Then that's on your personal list. Do you all think you need a mobile kitchen island? That goes on the group list.

- **Who is going to do the acquiring?** Decide if one of you will handle the purchasing/acquisition of said item, at which point it belongs to them and the rest have the right to use it while it is in the space. Or, if you'd rather all contribute to the cost jointly, you'll have to determine the optimum way to choose a single owner down the road.

- **How are you going to acquire said item(s)?** Here comes the motherly advice portion of our show—start with the cheapest option and work your way up to the option most comfortable for the group. *Getting it for free is a whole lot more satisfying than having to eat store brand cereal for dinner for a month to pay off just your share.* We'll discuss this one in more detail in a later chapter.

- **Logistics for getting it there. And inside. And will it fit?** First things first, you should know it fits before you even consider it. Period, the end. As for getting it there and inside, options range from friends and family to moving services. Again, start with the cheapest option and go from there.

- **Make a floor plan and play with furniture placement.** Don't forget to consider how these pieces get used. *It may be all well and good that the dining table and four chairs fit in the kitchen, but if there is no room to pull the chairs out to sit on them, then you have an issue.*

PROJECT: FLOOR PLAN SHUFFLE
- large workspace
- phone with photos, or photos printed out
- your bulletin board project from before
- measuring tape
- graph paper and pencils

Make it a party. Coffee and pastries or wine and charcuterie—whatever the guests and the time of day call for.

1. Plot out the space on the graph paper using each block as one square foot. Don't forget to account for windows, doors and which way they swing open, plus any other obstructions.

2. Measure the furniture you already have: the kitchen chairs from your mom, the bookcase you found free on the side of the road that just needs to be cleaned and painted, etc.

3. Either draw the footprint of the furniture on your graph paper in pencil or cut out paper to size so you can move them around.

4. Look at the photos you took and visualize the furniture in those spaces.

5. Are you happy with your decision? If yes, then great. If not, keep trying, all the while knowing the final decision may be that the piece you have in mind just won't work. *And better to know that before you move it in.*

TOTAL COST: FREE - $30 (depending on food and drink, and cost of printed photos)

* * *

Now, before you grab your coat and head to the nearest Homegoods, I'm going to ask you to take a beat. In the last chapter, I touched on forming your acquisition philosophy. In the next chapter, we'll go over where to buy what and how to make it work best for your needs. **But right now, if you haven't already, it's time to begin setting in motion your beliefs about possessions.**

I've been a home organizer for a long time, and I've seen firsthand the effects of long-term accumulation. It rarely ends well. Too much stuff leads to clutter-town, which is a few stops from disorganization-station, rounding the bend to overwhelmed-opolis, and your last stop is hoarder-ville. That's why I'm hoping to impart some words of wisdom to add to your packing list before your trip.

HOW TO BUY

- **Don't just buy to buy.** The thrill of shopping is a real thing. It produces all kinds of warm and fuzzy hormones and neurotransmitters like endorphins and dopamine. It's a quick fix of feeling good, that easily leads to addiction.

- **Don't buy "good enough."** You need a lamp and you have an idea of what you need and want in your head, but you just can't find it, or at least not in your price range. Unless you're going to be completely in the dark without one, don't buy anything if it's not something you actually want. You will never truly be happy with a make-do placeholder.

- **Don't fill your house all at once.** Unless you truly abhor shopping/decorating (which I find hard to believe since you're already deep into this book) you're going to want to add pieces over time. If you fill it all up, you risk cluttering it up when you buy something down the road.

Measure. Plan. Scrub.

WHAT TO BUY

- **Start with the big stuff first.** No sense buying that pencil holder before you have something to put it on. Useful furniture first, then occasional furniture, large decor, and lastly small decor. That means, desk and chair, followed by printer table, then rug, then something to hold pens and pencils.

- **Don't shop blindly.** Take the time to learn about what you are buying in retail stores. Things like what materials the product is made from, what warning labels, if any, it comes with, perhaps even the country of origin if you are concerned about the carbon footprint it produces by being transported. Depending on your position, you may want to delve further into a manufacturer's business practices. Sourcing items ethically and responsibly can be a rabbit hole, so don't let it overwhelm you. Just use it as a guideline to making informed decisions.

  NOTE: If a product has passed California health and environmental guidelines, it's super-safe. If not, it doesn't mean it's not safe, just not meeting the higher standards set in that state. Know that any product sold through a retail store has met the minimum safety guidelines for USA import.

- **Don't throw all your eggs in one shopping cart.** Please don't walk into a furniture store and say,

"I'll take example room 22. Wrap it up and deliver it to this address." Shop around. Research prices. Consider options. There are countless purchasing options available to you, from big box retail to yard sales, from online to custom-made. This is not life or death, so there is no rush. *And just my opinion, but matchy-matchy suites of furniture are dull. Choosing each piece on its own merits is far more satisfying.*

Since the single biggest reason people eventually become overwhelmed with their homes is owning too much stuff, then the solution must be just to not own too much stuff. Is it really that simple? Sort of, but since buying, getting, and having things are all activities that give us pleasure, not doing any of those things is an exercise in constant restraint. There must be a way to strike a balance, right? Indeed there is. **The secret is to get off the track of owning more than you can reasonably appreciate.**

What does that mean? Well, it doesn't mean that as long as you can cram it into your square footage, you're good. It doesn't mean that if you could potentially use it every once in a blue moon, it's a keeper. **What it means is that a given item holds value in your life and you appreciate its existence in your home on a regular basis.** Think about that for a second. Your favorite rubber spatula—the one you wash and reuse daily because it is perfect for making your morning omelette—is a must have. The waffle iron you only use when you host brunch, is something you might save. The fluted punchbowl your great aunt insisted you take, that doesn't fit in the cabinet and so has to sit on the counter, is a big question mark. Sure, it was nice of Great Aunt Libby to give you this beautiful heirloom that once belonged to her mother-in-law, but you have three square feet of countertop and half of it is devoted to something you will likely not use regularly, if ever. You can try to use it for something else—a sock bowl, maybe? Or you can discreetly decline until you have more room. If you can't use it, you are not appreciating it.

Let's look at this another way. Does this item you're considering have true value, or are you merely assigning value to it in order to possess it? And once you possess it, will it continue to hold value, or will its value depreciate the longer it is owned? It's heady stuff.

Before we get ahead of ourselves, let's pause this topic. We'll pick it up again in Chapter 3.

SCRUB

I'm going to make this one as simple as possible. **DO NOT MOVE YOUR THINGS IN UNTIL YOU HAVE SCRUBBED THE PLACE CLEAN.** Simple enough.

- **Make note of any issues** with the space and discuss with the landlord, management company, or owner. Things like stained floors, loose handles, leaking faucets. You want it known these issues predate you moving in. Then have them fixed if possible.

- Ask the landlord, or whomever else is in charge of handling issues, to **have the rental space professionally cleaned** before you move in.

- Regardless of whether or not they agree to provide cleaning, **clean it again,** either by hiring your own professional cleaners or by doing it yourself.

- **This is a heavy duty cleaning.** It will likely never be cleaned this thoroughly again. But who knows how many people have lived there before, or what their habits were. Best to do it now, before you have to work around your stuff.

- **Wash everything.** Floors, baseboards, air vents, windows, the pipes under the sinks, the bar inside the closet, in addition to the obvious items like the stovetop, oven, tub, and toilet. In a post-Covid world, this is not overkill. This is playing it safe AND setting the stage for your new life.

TOTAL COST for supplies: FREE - $30. (If you are short on cash, any dollar store has what you need. Or, ask your friends and family for castoff *cleaning supplies as a housewarming gift. If they are like I am, they will be more than happy to provide. Know this: Dish soap with antibacterial properties, a couple sponges, a scrub brush, baking soda, window cleaner, microfiber towels, and a handled plastic bucket will provide you the tools to clean almost anything. No need for name brands; they all do the same thing.)*

TOTAL COST for services: FREE - $200 (depending on the size and severity of the cleaning a crew will have to provide)

In summation:

1. **Measure your gut reaction, expectations, and square footage.**
2. **Plan ahead for what you need, make sure it will fit, and figure out what you have left to acquire.**
3. **Clean, scrub, disinfect. Your new life starts with this first home on your own.** ***Make sure the only dirt is yours.***

* * *

STORY TIME FROM BEFORE YOUR TIME

I've been lucky enough to have truly remarkable people enter my life. For a reason or a season these people often show me the power of moving forward from less than ideal circumstances. My friend William is one such example. After a period of recovery from addiction, he was looking to start a new life. He found his fresh start in a small town filled with artists and craftspeople—a welcoming community where he felt grounded in nature, surrounded with kindness, and inspired by the creativity of his new neighbors. He furnished his home with items handmade by local tradespeople or curated from the collections of antique dealers—no more than he needed to be comfortable, and each with a story. But the home itself held the greatest gift. It had previously been a stable, and was converted into shops on the first level and apartments above. He referred to his time there as "being stabled while becoming stable."

Why am I telling you this story? Choose your first home for what you need, for who you are, and for the person you hope to become. If you do, it will feed you in ways you could not have imagined.

3

Find Free Before Financing

I know the old people (myself included) are the primary users of Facebook these days, so it's not all that cool to be a part of it. **But you're not going to find a better place for free stuff near you than your local area's Buy Nothing page.**

BUY NOTHING

Buy Nothing is a Facebook group made up of people living in a common area, giving away stuff they own, for FREE. It is just as the name very succinctly states—you buy nothing. And this is not garbage stuff, either. I have gotten beautiful, like-new furniture, actual new-with-tags home decor, and fairly abused stone materials that I used in my garden. The positives of this process are many:

- The giver reduces clutter in their own home by downsizing items that no longer serve them.
- The giver makes room in their home without adding to the excess volume of landfills.
- The giver gives a second life to their possessions, thus creating added value and the feeling that their original purchase price is going farther.
- The giver gets the euphoria of goodwill and charity.
- The receiver finds something that fills a need they have.
- The receiver avoids purchasing something that does not require being in new condition (tools, garden equipment, sports equipment, etc.).
- The receiver can avoid purchasing items they only need a portion of (such as leftover paint or stain).
- The receiver is gifted an opportunity to stretch their creative muscle by refurbishing or repurposing older, unloved items.
- The receiver gains the pride of saving money, upcycling castoffs for their needs, and rescuing items from the dump.

The process works in reverse as well, since you can request items. Oftentimes, people don't even realize they have something of value to another person until there is a request for it. For example: one person posts to the group: "ISO (in search of) Large Moving Boxes." Another person remembers that they ordered more boxes than they actually used during their last move, and voila! New wardrobe boxes still in the shrinkwrap are out of my garage and on their way from Massachusetts to Ohio as I write this. Yes, that was me, hoarding those boxes in my garage because they were "new and I could still use them," when the truth is, by the time I used them they would have been so filled with dust and spiders, I'd probably just recycle them anyway.

* * *

Thanks to the **acquiring before buying** strategy, you now have the following items ready to move with you into your first home:

- Things you **already own** that you are taking with you.
- Things you are **being given by friends and family** from their own possessions. *"Thanks for the TV in my first apartment, Dad."*
- Things you have **collected from your local Buy Nothing page.** *Please keep that collection to just items you are going to use; this is not an occasion to ignite your hoarding tendencies.*
- Things you have **asked for on the Buy Nothing page** and received.

- BONUS: Things **left out at the curb with a FREE sign.** *I live in a college town, and for the entire months of May and September there are goodies just lying around waiting for new homes. Get 'em before it rains.*
  TOTAL COST: FREE/ZERO/GRATIS/ ON THE HOUSE

Do you have enough to make a start at living on your own, or are there still items you can't live without? If you've got unchecked boxes on your shopping list, **your next stop is buying secondhand goods.**

SECONDHAND OPTIONS

Yard sales, garage sales, tag sales, estate sales, auction houses, flea markets, thrift stores, charity shops, secondhand stores, consignment shops, vintage stores, antique stores, antique shows, Facebook Marketplace, eBay. **If someone owned it before you, whether it's used or still brand new, you can find it somewhere in the "previously owned" arena.** And there is no limit to the amount of goods in this marketplace. It boggles the mind that new products are manufactured at all when there is so much available at a fraction of the cost, just because it once belonged to someone else. All it needs is a little TLC, and sometimes not even that.

Are you wondering what the differences are between

all those secondhand purchasing options? Then let's go through them with some quick definitions.

- **Yard Sale:** sale of goods, typically set up in front of a home in the yard/driveway/garage area. Items are usually (but not necessarily) priced, and most are negotiable. Mostly household items and clothes, but can include bigger ticket items like furniture, refrigerators and sporting goods.

- **Garage Sale:** same as above. The name suggests it will go on rain or shine because of overhead cover.

- **Tag Sale:** same as above, with all items priced but still room for negotiation. This wording suggests higher price and quality.

- **Estate Sale:** typically held when a majority of a house's contents are for sale. Items remain staged in place and buyers have access to most if not all of the house. Typically run by an estate sale agent (who will take a percentage of the proceeds). Includes large furniture and other higher priced decor; may even include vehicles.

- **Auction House:** an auction can be run in-home in tandem with an estate sale, or items can be collected and sold off at the auctioneer's facilities or through the auctioneer's website. Items are assumed to be of greater worth, which is reflected in the starting bid and/or reserve price. Items are "won" either through silent or live auction when time expires or the auctioneer calls bidding closed, with the highest bid "winning". *I use quote marks because it's not free. You have "won" the right to pay for it.*

- **Flea Market:** typically a group of several vendors in a single location, selling on a regular basis. Most items are sold new and in bulk, but low overhead costs keep the prices down.

- **Thrift Store:** typically a large store that accepts product donations from the community and sells at a deeply discounted price. Revenue usually goes toward a charitable organization like Salvation Army or Goodwill.

- **Charity Shop:** usually a boutique-style shop that accepts and curates better quality product donations due to the limited space. Money earned goes directly to a local organization (church, school, hospital).

- **Secondhand Store:** a retail store where the shop owner purchases secondhand items to resell. Sometimes these items are upcycled, but they tend to be curated to the tastes of the shop owner. Not necessarily vintage or antique.

- **Consignment Shop:** can come in any shape and style, from children's clothing to high-end furnishings. Individuals contract with the store owner to sell their items on their behalf. Proceeds are paid on a percentage split (typically 60/40). Items that do not sell may be picked up by the original owner on a specific date or left to be donated.

- **Vintage Store:** typically a collection of individual vendors who rent a certain square footage in a larger space. Items for sale have either been purchased for resale or are from their own possessions, typically curated to a specific style or decade. May include antiques and collectibles. (To qualify for the wording "vintage" an item should be 50+ years old.)

- **Antique Store:** either an individual shop owner or a collection of vendors in a given space. Items for sale are typically higher quality, harder-to-find items with a higher price tag, such as furniture, jewelry, furs, rugs, and collectibles. (To qualify as an "antique" an item should be 100+ years old.)

- **Antique Show:** large event space rented for a specific number of days, where vendors from various locations set-up booths to sell their items. While it is called an antique show, items can run all ages and categories. Vendors are trying to recoup high rental fees in exchange for the potentially enormous number of shoppers who come out, so prices are high. Haggling is a given, especially on the last day when vendors are trying to sell off what's left.

- **Facebook Marketplace:** the ease of buying from your computer or phone, all in your local area for ease of pick-up or delivery. Pictures, prices, and condition are posted. Anything and everything is up for sale with no continuity, like an online yard sale without the seller having to sit outside all day.

- **eBay:** the OG of secondhand online sales, where you can buy and sell from all over the world. Be mindful of shipping costs and seller ratings that describe customer issues. Look for confirmation of factual photos and item descriptions.

Still think it's better to shop at Walmart? The secondhand marketplace is so clearly more plentiful and far more fun than buying some plastic doodad from a metal shelf in aisle 134A. It's like finding buried treasure!

* * *

I do want to caution you about the **previously owned** arena, though. The phrase "buyer beware" has never meant more than in this space. There are hidden flaws in abundance, rarely a return policy, and if you're not careful, it could wind up costing you more in the long run. There's a lot of crap out there; you're going to want to keep an eye out for some red-flag flaws, as well as some "Oh, Hell No" characteristics. On top of all that, you have your own impulses to keep an eye on. Ask yourself the following:

- Do you actually need it, or are you just drawn to the low price tag and the idea of reclaiming something from the trash?
- How much work will go into making it usable for your needs and space?
- Do you have the money, time, space, and skills to accomplish what needs to be done?
- Is it out of your price range even at second-hand prices?
- Do you think it's cool in the store and think to yourself, "I'll find a place for it," even though you don't need it?
- Will it actually work for you, either practically or aesthetically?
- Can it be shined-up...*or is it just sh*t?*

My life is nothing if not a tapestry of mistakes. My books speak to that very topic in great length. And while I think mistakes are the only true way we learn anything, I'm going to show you how to avoid the ones I've made. Grab your favorite stuffed guy, 'cause it's storytime.

* * *

It was 1998, and my then husband and I had just moved to Annapolis, Maryland, from New Jersey. I was exploring the shops in town when I spied a little occasional table at a beautifully curated furniture consignment warehouse. Sadly, the store is no longer there. Also sadly, that piece is no longer in my home. It has long since been sold at a yard sale for a fraction of what I put into it. But I'm getting ahead of myself. **Here are my mistakes, in order:**

- Mistake 1: buying something I didn't need to solve a problem I didn't have
- Mistake 2: attempting to restore it myself without thinking through my space and my skill set
- Mistake 3: sending it to a furniture restorer in order to strip it, paying them four times the amount I paid for the table in the first place
- Mistake 4: not having them just finish the job, because I still wanted to 'have another go at it'
- Mistake 5: having another go at it and screwing it up
- Mistake 6: making due with what I had done and begrudgingly placing the piece in my home
- Mistake 7: realizing my first mistake was actually purchasing a piece of furniture too small and dainty to be useful

- Mistake 8: keeping it in my house for years as a form of punishment for making all those previous mistakes
- Conclusion to the saga: finally selling it for a third of the original purchase price, not recouping any of what I spent on restoring it

For some reason which still eludes me, this pointless diminutive demilune console table, no more than 24" high and 18" wide, caught my eye and I was compelled to rescue it from obscurity in this massive secondhand warehouse. "I'll fix you up and give you a good home," was apparently my mindset.

ORIGINAL COST: $15

I took it home, dusted it off, and immediately jumped into painting it with leftover paint on hand. No sanding, no priming, no repairing the obvious wiggle in one leg. To add to the errors, in my infinite wisdom, I did this project in my new kitchen with no drop cloth, thinking "I'll be neat." And one final moron move, I used a thick paint roller I already had, instead of running out to the store for the proper paint brush. "It'll be fine," I presumably said to myself.

ADDITIONAL COST: FREE,
BUT NOT FOR LONG

I hated the way it turned out. And there was paint on my new kitchen floor. And it wouldn't sit flush against the wall because of the loose leg. Frustrated with myself but refusing to give up, I searched the Yellow Pages *(it was the olden days)* for a nearby furniture restorer to now not only strip what I had done, but prep it, so that all I had to do was decorate it. I cleaned up my mess, dropped off the table, and went home like nothing had ever happened.

ADDITIONAL COST: WASTED TIME & ENERGY, AGGRAVATION

A week later I retrieved my now stripped tiny half-moon table. It was handed to me in a shopping bag, in parts, with the screws in a little brown paper bag. It had been stripped, repaired, and prepped.

ADDITIONAL COST: $60/ TOTAL COST THUS FAR: $75

It sat in the bag for another week. I had become disgusted with it, and more so with myself. The worst part for me was that it was a pointless piece of nothing that I didn't need for any purpose. I had already spent $75 and I still couldn't use it. I should have had them just finish it, but "Nooo! I wanna do it!" I can hear myself saying, like some petulant child.

ADDITIONAL COST: SELF-LOATHING

Let's skip to the end, because just writing this story is raising my blood pressure. Years later, after a shoddy paint job and a move to Silver Spring, Maryland, where our yellow lab Hepburn knocked into it daily because it was in the worst possible location, I sold it at a yard sale. And I was happy to see it go.

SALE PRICE: $5…OR WHAT AMOUNTS TO 7% OF WHAT I SPENT ON IT.

Do not make the same mistakes I did.

* * *

But please wait, I don't want to scare you off of secondhand purchases entirely. I went into my first furniture rehab all wrong. With time, I learned a thing or two, and now can present you with the following step-by-step guide to handle the situation correctly and happily.

- **Know what you need, or at least what you really, really want.** You find a beautiful farm table that is exactly what you envisioned owning, so you're willing to pay the sticker price even though it's over budget. The problem is, your apartment only has room for a table that fits four people, not 12.

You are afraid you will never find this table again when you do have the room sometime in the future, so you are considering buying it anyway and storing it.
STOP
Firstly, that doesn't solve your need for a dining table now. Secondly, it costs more than you have. Thirdly, where are you going to put it until you can use it sometime in the future? Instead, tell yourself the truth: that *a table just like this one will be available when you need it. Go buy something you can use now. And stay on budget.*

- **Measure your space—height, width, depth.** You have found what appears to be the perfect armoire. You need it because you have more clothes than closet space, and you've already downsized your wardrobe as far as you're willing to go. It costs less than you thought and you like the wood, so all you need to do is clean and polish it. You assume it will work in the space by holding your arms out and guesstimating. It's heavy, so you're going to need help bringing it up the two flights of stairs into your apartment, but you know in your heart it will be worth it because this armoire is a forever piece.
WAIT
Have them hold it for you so you can take proper measurements. Better yet, measure before you go—both the space and the path to get it there.

What you've forgotten using the arm length method of measuring is that door jambs and oversized furniture don't always play nice, and that since this is an antique, modern hangers may be too wide to fit inside. *Take a tape measure with you to measure the pieces you find. Do not be distracted from practicality in pursuit of pretty.*

- **Lastly, if you don't find what you are looking for, keep looking.** Never buy anything just to fill a gap, even if it's something you need. You will only ever feel like it's not quite right. And the more you fill your home with "it-will-do-for-now" furniture, the more you will treat your home as temporary. That feeling of being unsettled in one's home, even short term housing, is one you should never permit yourself to feel. It breeds dissatisfaction, resentment, frustration, and depression. *Bottom line, don't get the demilune console table. Even if it's free, it costs too much of your energy.*

- **BONUS: Don't buy anything in the secondhand marketplace that is made of fabric, unless it can be washed in a washing machine.** Table linens? You can always buy these. Window treatments? Most of the time. Rugs? Occasionally. Decorative pillows? Hmm, maybe. Upholstered furniture/mattress/futons? Never. Again, if you can't wash it in a super hot heavy duty wash cycle of your standard home washing machine, god knows what is on it, and more importantly, in it. *Those items, you should buy NEW.*

* * *

What else should you buy new? Well, that depends on you. Personally, I will only ever purchase sheets and towels new from the store. Yes, I come down hard on people who say they won't eat off thrift store silverware by reminding them that restaurants don't pull out new utensils every time they dine, so why won't I buy secondhand sheets and towels when I know that when I go to a hotel, theirs have been used countless times? My answer is "because." We each have an ick factor. Maybe your ick factor is forks and maybe someone else's is books; this is why I say it depends on you. *(Yes, I have a friend who will not take out books from a library because they think the whole idea is gross.)*

Regardless of what your filth trigger is, my advice is to save up all those nickels you accumulated from buying mostly thrifted items, and splurge on good quality basics that will serve you well. Like a new couch or overstuffed chair and ottoman...or sheets and towels.

"So Bonnie, if you're telling me there are times to buy new, why go to all the trouble of hunting and cleaning and repairing and upcycling someone else's castoffs, when I can just get new low-cost furniture anywhere, at any time, and not have to do anything to it except put it together, and even then, not in all cases?" Ah, that's the million dollar question, isn't it? And here is my reply:

Because you, my dear, are not entering a world where the human race can afford yet another generation who doesn't pay attention to what's happening around them, like climate change, pollution, labor practices, and landfills (and those are just issues touched by furniture and home decor manufacturing). Nor will most of you be in the enviable situation of having discretionary funds for excess spending on temporary furnishings after paying college loans, rent and utilities, food price inflation, and gas prices, dealing with and the lack of job availability. You've got to make a change, and change begins at home.

* * *

TIME TO CHANGE THE WORLD...AND YOURSELF

That change must start with you and your mindset. This simple shift in perspective will be the difference between saving money or not, changing the planet or not, living with clutter and chaos or not, being happy or not. And what is that change? **Being, having, and living a life of <u>enough</u>.**

> "Do you want to go shopping?"
> "No thanks, I don't need anything."

> *"Should we purchase a new kitchen table?"*
> *"No, I think we can work with what we have."*
>
> *"Let's buy bathroom organizers to keep it neat."*
> *"Let's downsize what we don't use. Then there'll be less to keep organized."*
>
> *"I'm tired of being broke. I want to treat myself to something nice."*
> *"Ice cream is nice! We could check out that new gelato place."*

That last one is an inside joke with my daughter. Just ask her how many times a week this past summer I suggested we go out for ice cream, to which she replied, "we have ice cream." *I may have taught her too well about living with less.*

But that right there is the cornerstone of this profound change in your life…and, for the purposes of this book, your things. **You have to alter your attitude about possessions, both acquiring them and possessing them.** You don't need luxuries to feel luxurious. Think of all the good that comes from being more monastic with your attitude towards your home. I can repeat them all again but I'm starting to sound like a broken record. Okay, I'll say it anyway…

- **You will save money.** Secondhand furnishings are typically less expensive by A LOT than even cheap new items, plus they are usually better made. (Particleboard furniture manufacturing took off in the 1950s. Anything made previous to that was hardwood and more skillfully created.)

- **You will save a castoff from the dump, which in turn helps the environment.** Not only will you prevent a piece of used furniture from entering the overburdened landfills, you will also be helping the environment twice. Once an item enters the landfill there is a lengthy list of possible toxins released into the soil, water, and air. And, there is the additional pollution created by the manufacturing of fast furnishings. *It is my hope that the need and allure of such production will decrease as more people opt for acquiring used pieces.*

- **You will stretch your creative muscle and have a story to tell all at the same time.** As painful as my previous story of the demilune side table was, I have a hundred more success stories of reclaiming castoffs and making them my own. *Walking into a designer showhouse and buying a Henredon living room suite, as absolutely beautiful and elegant as they are, will only give you bragging rights about the enormous price tag you paid, not a tale of salvation and artistic endeavor.*

* * *

You Don't Need It

Everything around us is set up for consuming the "new and improved," the "on trend," the "latest in," and *if I don't wait in line for it at 2am is it even worth owning?* The glossy photos of celebrity homes give us a look into the aspirational world of the rich and famous, but that's not what draws our envy. We regular people don't ever expect to live that way. It's the ads for the attainable look on the shelves of every chain store that entices us to buy. Think of a trend in the last ten years and you'd be hard pressed to find one that couldn't be recreated with accessories from any multi-location behemoth. That's the true temptation.

But I'm veering slightly off topic. Let me get back on track. I was talking about envy and the wanting of things we don't need because we don't want to feel poor. We want to feel like we don't concern ourselves with money, that we have so much money we can shop with abandon. Believe me, I get it. I've been there. On some days when I'm feeling weak, I'm still there. Well, you might think that opening a credit card is the solution. You're young and you've got time to pay it off, right? **The answer is no. Never go into debt attempting to buy self-worth.** Because here's the sad truth: the treats you allow yourself in order not to feel deprived and mentally poor will keep you financially poor. And just for good measure, let me just mention that a good chunk of the stuff people are giving away in the "once owned/previously loved" marketplace were initially their "treats." That's how short-lived trying to buy happiness lasts.

Want bred from discontent works **two ways.** It leads to **boredom**, which takes the form of shopping. Or, **resentment** of what your friends have which makes you feel "less than." (There is also a third option that I see far less in your generation than the ones that have come before, and that is a "checklist of items one must acquire for a successful life." At one point that was hardwired into our culture.)

If it's boredom that plagues you, that's a simple enough fix. Find something else to do. Preferably something cheap or free. Bonus points if it also solves another issue, like exercising or charity work.

If it's resentment, then you have some internal work to do. The honest truth is that you can't buy self-worth, and owning things will never make you feel better about yourself. *I used to work in wholesale giftware sales, and I can almost guarantee that there is a local gift shop near you selling a wooden sign with calligraphy written on it that says "Treat yourself! You are worth it." And while that is, literally, one way to buy self-worth, I'm going to suggest you not purchase that little dust collector and instead treat yourself by feeling worthy just because you are.*

If it's the checklist, the one that says "graduate from college, get a high paying corporate job, get married, buy a house and fill the house with things, have children, etc." I'm going to warn you that **happiness**

does not necessarily lie in that direction, either. True happiness will only ever come from intangible things like self-love, confidence, self-worth, and living a fulfilling life of your choosing. Not in buying a luxury car you can't afford to make you look like you can.

Here is where things get more complex. Even if you could buy whatever it is you are looking to buy, there is a chance you'd still feel as if it wasn't good enough. There's an old quote by Groucho Marx that illustrates this point: "I wouldn't want to belong to a club that would have me as a member." *I pulled that from the internet, so I'm 100% certain that's not the actual quote, but the gist is there.* In a nutshell: if I can afford it, it must not be that good. Let me dissuade you from that thought here and now. If you live with that mindset, you will ALWAYS and FOREVER be unhappy. Why? Because there is always going to be someone with more than you. "Better" than you. Always. Look at the current richest person in the world. They have everything money can buy, right? Are they happy? They are nearly universally disliked, so you tell me. Sounds like a pretty empty life. No matter how filled with toys it may be.

So what am I getting at, you ask? **If you believe that what you were given, what you found, and what you were able to buy are nothing but lousy castoffs, unwanteds, and cheap crap, then you are going to treat them and yourself the same in turn...**

like rotten garbage. I'll give you an example by way of a story.

* * *

After the publication of my first book, *Stop Buying Bins*, I had quite a few people reach out to me by DMing me through Instagram. I received messages from readers as far as California and Texas, to South Carolina and Virginia, and a few right here in Massachusetts. They had questions about their living situation and asked if I would mind helping them with some guidance. I was happy to help and always started with the same request: would you send me photos of the space in question? Not surprisingly, the clutter took all forms, from mildly messy to "why would you willingly send me those pictures?" What I found in nearly all cases was a lack of respect for their things. *Lots and lots of things.* All of which were being abused because "We're not fancy. Nothing we own costs that much, so we can replace them when they get too beat up." ***Sigh** It's not about fancy. It's about fulfillment.*

It boggles my mind that anyone would live with that mentality. It's so hurtful, not just to your personal environment but to your mood. It's sad and depressing, if you want to know the truth, and **it's no wonder at all to me why certain homes are complete disasters. It's because the occupants are treating themselves and their stuff like trash.**

SIDE STORY: I was once in discussions with one of these people who contacted me on Instagram, and when I mentioned that she may not be finding her momentum to handle the task because she doesn't feel it's worth it, she said, no lie, "It's not. Everyone keeps telling me to hire someone. I thought I could hire you because you're not far. But I don't really care what my house looks like." Oh, how I wanted to reply, "Then why are you wasting my time?!"

* * *

We've covered a lot of topics in this chapter, so to sum up, here are the **"Things I Am Strongly Advising You To Do During This Period of Acquisition"**:

- Make this a true home. One you love, surrounded by the people and moments that make you happiest.

- Graciously accept any useful donations from family and friends. If they are not exactly to your taste, you will alter them to your style.

- Be grateful, but decline any offered items you know will not be of service to you, so as not to continue the cycle of holding onto things you have been burdened with.

- Stick to an acquisition list, so as not to over-accumulate and clutter.

Find Free Before Financing

- Measure your space and the physical path these items need to take in order to get there.
- Stick to a cash budget. This is not the moment to rack up credit card charges.
- Keep an eye out for giveaways and FREE items.
- Make secondhand shopping an activity that brings you more joy than buying and owning.
- Don't buy just to buy; wait for the right piece.
- Take into consideration your workspace, time available, materials needed, and access to tutorials to improve your skill set, before taking on any upgrading projects.
- Only take on one project at a time.
- If you do not have the time for a project in the immediate future, pass. There will be others.
- If the season and weather will be inappropriate to working on a project, skip it. There will be others.
- Don't over-shop just because the price is low. This is not a time to strengthen your hoarding gene.
- Don't buy everything all at once. *One of my greatest joys is finding things I fall in love with in my travels.*

- Don't buy quantities for future use *(unless we are talking about toilet paper)*.
- Don't buy with "temporary" in mind. Buy quality always. *And not to get ahead of myself, but instilling this idea in yourself now will hopefully instill this idea in your children, who may one day fight over who gets that cherry china cabinet that has been painted, stripped, and stained, had glass doors removed, then put back on, had feet added, then taken off to fit a smaller space… all because you bought an unloved piece of secondhand furniture that was built with quality materials in an old-school way to withstand the test of time, and not some mass produced, machine-made-out-of-particle-board product that you had to assemble yourself from a box. Yeah, no one's fighting over that one.*

* * *

Whew. Anyone else feeling excited to hit the antique mart or scan the Buy Nothing pages with me? That is, of course, if I actually needed anything, which I don't, so I won't. I'll treat myself to a home-brewed coffee while gazing at my pottery collection instead. *(Most of which I bought at the thrift store.)*

* * *

STORY TIME FROM BEFORE YOUR TIME

In preparing to write this book, I asked friends to give me their "first home" stories. The good, the bad, and the downright ugly. And because they are my friends (some whom I've known for 40 years), they gave me all the dirty details willingly. From roommate horror stories to nasty landlords to questionable couches "left for their use," I have more than enough for a few more books. But there was a common thread—you can't go wrong with a little imagination…and a flat sheet. More than one friend touted the versatility of the humble square of cloth in making their spaces not only more livable but also more lively. From window treatments to table clothes, from wall hangings to covering that scary sofa, any sheet or piece of fabric can change the grotesque to the gorgeous. Whether you get it from the linen closet in your parents' home, the thrift store, or Amazon, you can do any number or things with a flat sheet. Ask any adult in your life. They've all used one for something other than making their bed. *Do people still host toga parties?*

Part 2:

THE FIRST SIX MONTHS

4

Keep Organizing In Mind

Repairs have been made, walls have been painted, and the place has been deep cleaned. Move in day has come and gone, and you're surrounded by boxes and bags piled high and furniture left scattered in odd locations. Nothing is in place, you can't find the light switch, and last night you slept on your mattress on the floor with a towel for a blanket. Ahh, your first home. Now what?

- **Be prepared**
- **Consider your space**
- **Empty your boxes**

BE PREPARED

You're standing in the middle of a mountain of boxes and you're thinking to yourself, "OK, what do I do first?" The answer is toilet paper. What? You heard me right. You're not going to want to be ripping through taped cardboard when you have "to go." In fact, let's back up a bit so I can tell you about the number one best idea ever in the history of moving: **A MOVE-IN BOX.** Separate from the rest of your things, have a box filled with the essentials needed for a smooth unpacking process:

- A roll of toilet paper
- A roll of paper towels
- Basic toolbox—*details below for the ideal starter toolbox*
- Bottled water
- Scissors and/or boxcutter
- Paper and pen
- Large trash bags
- Soap and/or antibacterial hand sanitizer
- Band-aids and first aid cream
- Pain medication (Advil, Tylenol, etc.)
- Snacks
- One set of towels
- One set of sheets
- Blanket and pillow
- Basic toiletries (toothbrush, toothpaste, deodorant, etc.)
- A change of clothes
- You can also pack a pot and some canned food, but I expect you'll want to eat out until

you are fully unpacked, <u>so budget for that.</u> It also gives you a chance to check out your new neighborhood.

This list is pretty self-explanatory. Your starter kit will make the unpacking process so much easier by covering some necessary basics. Pack it all in a plastic bin, then once the bin is empty you can use it as a recycling container for all those empty boxes and packing materials you will amass. A starter kit just makes life easier, and **ease is exactly what you need during any move.**

Now set it all up. Did you put the toilet paper, towels, and toiletries in the bathroom? Did you make your bed? Do you have your box-breaking-down system in place? Great. **Take a break.** Yes, you can actually stop here for the moment while you have some daylight, because you are at least covered for the basics. Take this opportunity to investigate your new building, block, neighborhood, city. Find all those places you will likely use down the road, from pizza to parking. **Your best chance of loving where you live is to invest your time in truly taking advantage of all it has to offer.**

* * *

I hope you put this book down and ran to the nearest deli to grab some lunch, then window shopped (which is really only looking) along the main street, before checking out the local gym. It's all part of leaning into this experience of living on your own. Perhaps in your travels you discovered a local hardware store? Get to know the staff; they will be an invaluable resource for repairs and projects down the road.

PROJECT: YOUR IDEAL STARTER TOOLBOX
- 16"-20" heavy duty plastic toolbox, preferably with tray that has compartments for small items like screws and nails *COST: $13-$30 depending on features, brand, and retailer*
- the aforementioned measuring tape from the chapter "Measure. Plan. Scrub." *COST: $10-$30*
- claw hammer *COST: under $10*
- screwdrivers (both flathead and Phillips, and maybe even a Robertson, in different head sizes) *COST: set of 10 for under $30*
- pliers (both needle-nose and side cutter or combination pliers, *though truthfully, my needle nose pliers get by far the most use) COST: set of 5 for under $20*
- wrench (adjustable) *COST: under $15*
- level *COST: under $10*
- black electrical tape *COST: under $5*
- picture-hanging kit *COST: under $10*
- self-adhesive bumper feet in plastic and felt (assorted sizes) *COST: under $10*

- Gorilla Glue or Super Glue *COST: each under $10*

The above are new prices, and probably a bit more money than you'd like to spend. Ask your family, ask your neighbors, ask online for free or cheap hand tools others are willing to part with. Yard sales are another good place to look, but get there early, as tools usually go first. It is absolutely essential you have a toolbox and tools. You will never regret having spent good money on these necessities that you will use for the rest of your life.

SIDE STORY: I have added to my toolbox over the years but I still have all the original hand tools from my first box, including the box. What I now deem essential in the course of my work are a heavy duty electric staple gun (mostly used for upholstering), and an electric drill with various drill bits and screws (for so many tasks, it's immeasurable.) Rechargeable battery tools are an excellent option so as not to be tethered to a cord and outlet, but they are significantly heavier to handle than wired tools. When you get to that point in your tool acquisition, choose what works best for you.

CONSIDER YOUR SPACE

Now that you are back in your new digs with a bit of energy left to keep moving, let's get back on track. **This**

is the time to consider how your home will function best. Moreso, this is the time to set yourself up for continued success when it comes to cleaning and organizing—habits that will serve you for a lifetime.

Think about the "work spaces" you need:
- a place to sleep
- a place to eat
- a place to watch TV
- a place to work
- a place to store clothes, food, and cleaning supplies

Depending on the size of your first home, all those places may actually be one space.

Let's say you have a two bedroom apartment you share with a roommate. You are not quite friends yet and have different social groups, but you've worked out a nice arrangement to divide the days and times you work and entertain. You work from home two days a week and your roommate works early mornings and evenings as a trainer at a local gym, so they are generally home during the day. You plan to have friends over on Thursday nights for pizza plus your favorite TV show. Your roommate has their book club meetings on Tuesday nights with wine and charcuterie. You are each welcome to the others. And every third Saturday of the month you've decided to have a potluck dinner party with both groups of friends.

The apartment takes up the top floor of a brownstone. It has a galley kitchen without a dining area, so a table and chairs will have to be placed in the common living space. Both the kitchen and living room are in the back of the house. You each have a good-sized walk-in closet in your separate surprisingly large bedrooms, which are both at the front of the house. And you share a reasonably large windowless bathroom, which is situated in the center of the house.

You may think all of this discussion doesn't matter when you are planning where to put what, but you would be wrong. All of it must be considered when contemplating the natural flow of your space. Because while you have the luxury of taking your time to set-up your individual bedrooms on your own, the two of you have to work together on common areas. These spaces have to:

- Serve the way you live (dining space, TV, desks, reading, individual space in shared space like common closets)
- Combat any structural issues with the space (outlets, sunlight, door frames, radiators, built-ins)
- Setup your new home for both ease of movement and efficiency for cleaning and organizing (not tripping over or walking around items, having things where you use them)

If you are lucky enough to have your own place, feel free to have piles of whatnot strewn about with no regard for how inconvenient or frustrating it is to maneuver around them. Though, I would advise against cultivating those habits. It won't serve you to live like that, ever.

As you are putting things in place, keep these two thoughts in your mind.

1. **Organize first, decorate after.** If your home does not function, no amount of finery or fluff will make it look good.

2. **True home organization is not about perfect rows with the labels turned out.** It's about workability.
    - → **Set up user-friendly systems that create efficiency.**
    - → **Make stored items readily available.**
    - → **Provide habits built on muscle memory for exactly where everything is.**
    - → **Be able to know when you are running low on something and need to replenish.**
    - → **Reduce clutter accumulation or overbuying because you have lost track of how much you have.**

    And you thought it was just for the Instagram photo. #organizationporn

In thinking about how to proceed with this chapter, I was thinking about my first apartment's bathroom, and the bathroom I have now, and every bathroom I've had in between. *I have a thing for bathrooms.* Each one is different; a fact that makes giving specific advice difficult. Some of you will have a medicine cabinet, some wall shelves, or under sink drawers and storage, or a linen closet in the bathroom. Others will have enough empty space for some piece of furniture to serve your needs, or all of the above...or none of the above. So what should I say to make the process of setting up a well-organized bathroom (or any room) easy for you to follow? **Here is the SIMPLE TRUTH about organizing—organizing makes sense! It's that easy.**

So since we are on the subject, let's get into that bathroom. It's the most important room in the house, plus it's usually the smallest and therefore quickest to complete. In all cases where you are not custom-building a home, you don't get to decide where things are built-in and believe me, you will find things in the strangest places *(see my side story below)*. But let's get back on topic. Consider how you use a space, and then build around your needs/habits. Things like:

- Putting items where you use them. Example: soap and hand towel near the sink.

- Placing back-up supplies within convenient reach or retrieval. Example: extra rolls of toilet paper within reach when you run out *while using the toilet.*

- Take into account the ease of motion to reach for these items as well as what it takes to put them back. Example: Is the towel bar across the room from the shower? Not ideal.

- Consider the space's attributes as part of the practicality or detriment. Example: hanging towels above the baseboard radiator makes for warm and cozy towels; it also makes for a good fire-starter if the towel touches the coils.

See what I mean about having it all make sense by considering how you use it? So as you formulate your plan for each room, don't just look at the space and say, "There is no soap holder by the sink. I guess we'll just have to use the one in the shower to wash our hands." Put a soap dish/dispenser near the sink. It's that simple. Which is an excellent segue into my side story.

SIDE STORY: I was working with a realtor in Hoboken on the hunt for my first apartment. One of the apartments I was shown was huge, if not a bit quirky. Quirky as in the refrigerator was in an adjacent room to the kitchen. Another quirk was in the bathroom. The wall-mounted sink did not have a vanity, and so it was not large enough to hold a bar of soap. Instead, there was a soap dish mounted to the wall. This would be all well and good were it not for the fact that the wall below it was wet and covered with soap scum, as was the floor underneath. In fact, there was no real way to make the process of washing your hands and face any less messy with the dish where it was. *And for me personally, at five feet tall, it was attached so high on the wall that I would have to reach up for it. I couldn't get past the idea of soap and water running down my arm into my clothes. That was one quirk too many for me.* I passed on the bigger apartment for a studio with fewer quirks.

While we are still in the bathroom, let's take a quick break for a project.

PROJECT: HANGING TOWEL LOOP
- any size towel
- coordinating fabric ribbon in twill or grosgrain
- nylon thread
- heavy duty hand needle, or sewing machine

I love this project. It's ideal for beach towels so they don't slip off hooks in public bathrooms, but also perfect for bathrooms with more than one occupant. Everyone is assigned a hook and every towel hangs the same.

1. Find the center of the long side of the towel.
2. Cut a 6" piece of ribbon.

3. Pin both ends of the ribbon together to the center of the long side of the towel, creating a loop.
4. Sew in place, going back and forth several times for strength.
5. Hang on hook from loop.

TOTAL COST: FREE (if you have all the supplies on hand) - $10 (ribbon/thread)

And while we're talking towels, let's discuss how to keep them hung instead of flung over the shower curtain bar.

TUTORIAL: Hanging something on the wall is so much more than hammering in a nail. It depends on what you're hanging, for one. And into what kind of surface, secondly. A lightweight framed photo that you hang and only ever touch with a feather duster does not require a heavy duty metal wall anchor and a lag screw (yes, I had to look up what the screw I envisioned in my head was called). Likewise, a bath towel cannot be hung on a tack, or you will be picking that towel up off the floor after every shower. So, here is a quick wall-hanging lesson for you.

- Wood surface: any common nail or screw; screws provide more strength and stability. Depending on the size and weight of what you are hanging, use two nails horizontally a few inches apart (use your level). This is not because one nail won't hold it, but because two nails will prevent it from swinging like a pendulum if it gets bumped. Bear in mind that if you use more than one nail, you will shorten how far it hangs by picking up slack in the hanging wire on the frame.

- Drywall surface: screw and anchor (metal or plastic) or picture hanger hook. The strength of the screw/anchor combo depends on what you are hanging and if it is something that gets used. Think wall art versus coat hook. Picture hanger hooks are an excellent option for hanging stationary objects, since they are easy to install and depending on size can hold up to 100lbs.

- Tile surface: DO NOT ATTEMPT to install into ceramic or clay tile; especially as a renter. Hooks and hangers that use suction, Velcro, or removable sticky tape are your option here. Again, they vary in size and the weight they can hold.

- Cement surface: If you are a renter, DON'T even think about it. As an owner, consider it carefully before proceeding. You will need a drill with a masonry drill bit, and a specific anchor/screw combo designed for cement.

So, where should you install hooks for your towels in a bathroom? Either directly into wood beams or trim, or into a stud (using a stud finder) behind the drywall. Your other option is to use a heavy duty anchor/screw combo into the drywall, but even at its best, the constant use of these hooks will cause the anchor to come loose over time. If the bathroom is entirely tiled, your options will be limited to suction, adhesive, or Velcro hooks. However, if you use them and find they can't bear the weight of a wet towel, you might consider the last option of finding a stand-alone towel rack to fit what could be limited bathroom space. While you're at it, if there are not sufficient towel holders (and by sufficient, I mean one for each member of the household) add them to the shopping list. No one should ever have to share a towel bar or hook. It's unsanitary on several levels, not the least of which is that your towel will never get fully dry between uses if it's bunched up next to someone else's.

Man, all this just to hang up a towel? That seems like a lot of work. Only at first, and then it's easy-peasy ever after. Your towels are within reach when you need them. They are separated from your housemates'. They have room to dry between showers. And the room always looks neat. It's worth the initial brainstorming.

EMPTY YOUR BOXES

Remember earlier in the chapter, I told you about this imaginary apartment you share with a roommate? Let's tackle the living room and kitchen next as a duo, because that's where the bulk of the entertaining as well as just living are going to be taking place. You've got a couple issues to consider: there is no seating area in the galley kitchen, the stairs up to your apartment come right into the living space, the largest wall in the room is exposed brick and has a fireplace that juts out into the room (it is boarded up and not legal for use), there are two large windows out the back, one overhead ceiling light/fan in the center of the room, and only one electrical outlet per wall. Now…go!

Just kidding! I wouldn't leave you without giving you some guidance. Of course, you'll want to make all the decisions on your own, as you should, but I want to give you my two cents on what to consider as you unpack and set-up. **One, place your furniture with practicality in mind, and two, as you begin to live in your space, determine if the placement is workable.** Here are a few examples of what I mean:

- Logically, your dining table and chairs should be nearest to the kitchen, but how you place them is more important than where. Are the dining chairs far enough from obstacles like walls and other furnishings so that you can get in and out of your seat easily without hitting something?

- Assuming you are using electronics at your workspace, your desk or work table will need to be near outlets for devices and lamps. Ask yourself if cords are neat and tidy. Likewise, are they long enough to reach from where you sit to the outlet with ease?

- Bookcases should be placed against solid walls, and if they are tall, consider anchoring them to the wall. Once you've filled the bookcase with books, does it feel secure or unstable when you remove and put back books?

- Do not place bar-carts (with alcohol) near direct light or heating sources. *Bar carts with plants can certainly be in direct light but not near heating sources.*

- Would you like to place a lamp more in the middle of the room? If you have no outlet in the floor for this purpose, secure the cords using coordinating duct or electrical tape and run it parallel to the cord. Tape down tightly. Place an area rug over the cord for added trip prevention.

- Speaking of rugs, use non-slip pads with all rugs. And weight down corners while you wait

Keep Organizing In Mind

for it to uncurl from the move. Do you keep tripping over the corners even after weighing it down for a few days? Rug tape or rug corners will do the trick.

Even after everything is in place, do you feel like you have to walk around pieces of furniture instead of having a natural pathway through the room? Make adjustments accordingly for better flow, telling yourself that it may require removing something altogether.

So what about that apartment? With those big windows, fabrics will fade in the sun, and during certain times of day it might be difficult to see the TV. Bear these things in mind as you set up. Hang wall decor properly based on wall materials (see instructions above), and if you have to anchor a bookcase, that brick wall might not be the best choice. Always be thinking about how your items get used. You never want to continuously have to move something out of the way to get to something else you use regularly. That item should be easily accessible. Likewise, put items where you use them—the TV remote belongs near the TV, over mitts near the oven. That system applies tenfold as you get into organizing your kitchen—mugs where you make your coffee and tea, cooking utensils next to the stove. And in this apartment, where you have no eating area in the kitchen, decide if you will be serving plates out of the kitchen or family style from the dining table. The first way, you will want to have the dishes, bowls, etc. near the counter; the second, you will want them stacked near the table for setting.

Lastly, when it comes to problem solving, don't immediately "buy" your solution. What do I mean?

- Don't buy organizing systems for inside your cabinets and drawers if you have something on hand that can work just as well for how you live. *For example: there is nothing that says you can't have your silverware in pottery crocks on the counter instead of in a divider in a drawer.*

- Don't buy storage bins, when downsizing is what you really need to do. There is a fantastic book on that subject. Maybe you have heard of it. It's titled *STOP BUYING BINS.*

- And never buy the solution before the problem exists. *Meaning, if you don't drink wine, you don't need a wine rack or a wine fridge or an electric wine bottle opener charging on your countertop, taking up space.*

That should cover you. We'll talk more about decor and lifestyle systems in the coming chapters. For now, you've got guidelines to keep in mind as you follow through on your personal vision. There will be tweaks to be made. Know that upfront. Decorating, and moreso, organizing, is never a set-it-and-forget-it scenario. There is always room for improvement.

Don't forget to enjoy every minute of it!

BONUS DEFINITIONS: As you and your roommate discuss housework, you will want to differentiate between these various tasks:

- DECLUTTERING: getting rid of excess possessions and either repurposing them for use somewhere else in the home, selling them off, or giving them away. Also called downsizing. Should be done as often as needed or regularly, as with the change of seasons. The space may not be tidy, organized, or clean, but it is decluttered to a reasonable amount and now it can be tidied, organized, and cleaned effectively. Will result in more chaos first since it is step one in organizing.

- ORGANIZING: taking the remaining reasonable number of items you have and placing them in an orderly manner for the most user-friendly, task-oriented efficiency. Should be done once then maintained and tweaked for your needs going forward. Will result in a tidy but not necessarily clean space; cannot be accomplished well if space is not first decluttered.

- TIDYING: putting items back where were originally placed when the room was fully decorated and organized. Also called straightening. Should be done at the end of every day. A space can be tidy without being decluttered, organized, or clean. Things are off the floor and surfaces, and the room has the appearance of being neat.

- CLEANING: using products, solutions, and equipment to rid the space of dirt, dust, grime, pet hair, etc. The previous steps make cleaning easier and more efficient. Should be done daily, weekly, monthly, or annually depending on the task. Has little to do with decluttering or organizing per se, and doing the former will not automatically make the space clean.

* * *

STORY TIME FROM BEFORE YOUR TIME

Three of the friends I spoke with when writing this book had moved from their parents' homes into their marriage homes. One friend, in fact, still lives in that same house. One has moved several times, to several different states. The third one is about to move for the first time in a long time. All began their married lives with a clear plan in place for living together—who does what chore and what tasks get done together. Sharing your life with someone you love is not the same thing as sharing space with someone you live with, especially if you are very different in that regard. One's messy, one's neat. One's a morning person, one's a night owl. One doesn't know that dirty laundry goes in the laundry basket, not next to it; one wants to murder the first because of that. Setting clear ground rules for living can head off a multitude of obstacles with anyone you live with. Put a plan in place. Whether you split the chores by playing a zone *(I'd take laundry every time, if I had a choice)* or with a weekly schedule, living with someone means keeping up with your end of things out of respect. I can imagine that if I had lived with a roommate back in my first apartment, I would likely be the dish washer, dryer, and put-awayer in exchange for my roommate doing the cooking *(I don't love cooking)*. I would also willingly take on all the vacuuming, if it meant I didn't have to dust. If you are really in sync, you could do it all together as a team. There is nothing I appreciate more than seeing teamwork in action when it works. Probably because I'm not great at team activities. *(Guess that's why I live alone, haha.)* That is to say, make a plan, follow through, respect each other and your space.

5

Learn How To Live In Your Space

You've placed your furniture. You've emptied your boxes. You're eating, sleeping, and living in your own place. It's all great...

Except, you can't stand that your roommate leaves the living area a mess, with blankets strewn on the couch and dirty dishes on the coffee table, and let's add to that the toothpaste splatter on the bathroom mirror, just for good measure. But you've got to get to work and don't have time to clean it or even leave them a nasty note telling them to clean it. It begins a chain reaction where you eat your feelings and don't want to be in the apartment anymore. Unacceptable on both your parts!

Or, you had decided that Wi-Fi is roughly the same monthly cost as all the streaming platforms combined, so instead of each paying for half, you would each handle one. But then your roommate decides it's not worth it for them to pay for Hulu since they don't watch anything there, so they are going to drop it, leaving you wondering where you are going to watch "Only Murders In The Building" next season and fuming because they have reduced their monthly expenses and now the two of you are no longer paying equally. That should not happen!

And if it's come to that, you've got to make a change here and now!

Presumably, you had the discussion prior to moving in together about how chores would get done and bills would be paid. If you didn't, you are locked into a lease now, so instead of telling you to reread chapter one, which at this time is pointless, I'm instead going to say, **you've got to work this out, openly, honestly, and immediately.**

- **Schedule a time** that is comfortable for both of you and free of other plans that might make you rush the discussion.

- **Find a neutral location** outside of your home and then return to the home together to work through the practicalities.

- You will probably both be frustrated, maybe even angry, but you have to **agree to respect the other person** until you can stop living together *(if in fact it is that bad a situation* *and cohabitating past your lease date is off the table).*

- This will always be about mutual respect. Your roommate may be messy, but it's more than likely you possess an equally irksome trait that they have let go unspoken. **Don't assume you are in the right** completely *(as difficult as that may be).*

- Make the best of a bad situation by **agreeing to make it better**. So much good comes out of living with someone and working through your problems with maturity—for the short term certainly, but any lessons learned will serve you for a lifetime of relationships.

BEFORE THE MESS GETS OUT OF HAND, SET YOURSELF UP FOR SUCCESS

Before things with your roommate come to blows, set a process of success in motion. Even if things go awry, you will be able to get back on track with relative ease if there is a system in place underneath the mess.

- When you are opening boxes and putting things away for the first time, best to **keep your items separate.** Separate shelves, separate cabinets, separate coat hooks at the front door. Do this with as many things as you can before you start taping a line down the center of the room.

- Anything you planned ahead of time to share should be **treated with the utmost respect** by the non-owner. In other words, don't put a glass of water on top of your roommate's wood coffee table without a coaster even if the coffee table is previously marked. Bonus there is that even if your roommate doesn't care if you use a coaster or not, using one will create a good habit for you going forward for yourself and in other people's homes.

- Housework is a tough one. I mentioned before, you can split the task list or split the days you each do the task, but at the end of the day, everyone should feel like **tasks were handled with equality and accuracy.**

SIDE STORY: "Why did you wash *only your* bowl and spoon?"

"Isn't it easier if we each wash our own?"

"You mean you'll wash just the stuff *you* ate off of?"

"Yeah."

"Then who washes the pot the food was cooked in? And why would you dig out and wash just your stuff and leave a sink filled with other dishes? That's ridiculous!"

No it is not easier. It's inefficient, takes longer, and someone is always left cleaning up what wasn't deemed "someone's" responsibility. Either split the chores or split the days, but not the task. *And yes, this is an actual conversation I have had.*

Let's get back to setting up a system of ownership. Naturally, if you live alone you only need to set it up for yourself, but even then it's best to do it all for continued maintenance. As for the two or more of you living together it's time for a project, and if you are a life-at-right-angles weirdo, like me, this is going to be fun!

PROJECT: SETTING UP YOUR PANTRY *(assuming you have one and if not, we will discuss the alternatives afterwards)*

- For peace of mind and the prevention of arguments, keep your items separate. Do this by either having separate bins that share the same shelf, or different shelves altogether.

- Keep shared shelves (your side of the shelf/their side of the shelf) to common items—paper goods, canned foods, etc. If you live alone, food and cleaning supplies never go on the same shelf, for safety reasons. *"But Bonnie, why would I ever put them on the same shelf? That seems kinda dumb." Yes it is, and I've seen it more than once in homes of people who should know better.*

- While we're at it, cleaning supplies should be stored in a separate location, or at the very least as far from food as possible.

- Lightweight paper goods and oversized cereal boxes on top shelves. Labeled items, with labels turned out, at eye level shelves. Root vegetables like potatoes, onions, and garlic, placed slightly below eye level in open-topped containers (stored in the refrigerator once cut.) Heavy containers on lower shelves or the floor *so you don't risk them dropping on your head.*

- Let's talk about how to stack and store. Everything in your pantry is for ease of motion. You should be able to reach an item, pull it off the shelf or put it back on the shelf, without having to move several items out of the way or having items topple in the process. Let me give you some examples:
    → On the top shelf, stack your paper towel rolls on their side. Take from the top row first. If you place your paper towels upright, at some point you will have one or more rolls too far back on the shelf to reach and run into possibly rebuying before it is necessary.
    → On the shelf at eye level, keep cans, jars, and bottles with labels facing out so they are easier to read, smaller items near the front so they don't get lost, and items with later

expirations placed near the back of their size grouping. *As a side note: regularly go through your items and make a point of using them before they expire. Three-can recipes are readily available online and can be delicious!*

→ Ideally, cotton fabric-lined baskets are best for storing root vegetables. The open top and breathable container won't hold moisture, which contributes to faster rotting. Plus the washable liner provides an extra barrier from dirt or onion skins falling onto the shelf or floor. *If this is not something you need, then bonus for you—you have an extra shelf.*

→ Lastly, the bottom shelf or floor is perfect for large and heavy items in nonporous containers like aluminum, glass, or plastic. Things like large bottles of olive oil, white vinegar, gallon-size bottles of water, or cases of soda. *Alcohol and wine too, if you haven't created a space in your living area for that.*

- Those without a pantry can use cabinets in much the same way: lighter items in top cabinets, heavier items in lower cabinets. Paper goods tend to take up a lot of space, so consider that when shopping in bulk, and perhaps choose to stock only a few at a time.

- If you can't spare the cabinet space, there are creative ways to add storage for your needs, from small bookshelves to wall shelves and even rolling carts that double as kitchen islands. **But as always, have a need before you buy, and search your secondhand options first.** An old credenza that you clean, paint, and maybe add wheels to as well as roll-out shelves inside, gives you exactly what you need since you can tailor it to you. *Not to mention, serious bragging rights for creating such a unique piece!*

NOTE: Continually keep your storage areas clean by wiping drips off containers and spills on shelves when they happen. Pests are plentiful! Stay vigilantly on the lookout for signs of bugs and critters, then resolve and prevent accordingly, avoiding hazardous ingredients near your food of course. Traps and glue strips are best (though none are perfect if you think too much about it).

SIDE STORY: Back in my beloved Hoboken apartment I had two pest altercations. Both provided invaluable learning experiences that forever changed how I managed my homes.

The first was a few months in, I came across three water bugs in my bathroom. HUGE water bugs! Having never lived in an urban area, I assumed they were cockroaches, screamed my lungs out, promptly called my landlord, and moved in with a friend until it was taken care of. I have no idea what my landlord did but I never saw them again. After gearing myself in a homemade hazmat suit, inspecting every corner and closet, rewashing all my towels and sheets in hot water, and scrubbing the place top to bottom, I was once again comfortable living there. Turns out it had more to do with the standing water on the flat roof than my unopened boxes of soap, but I wasn't taking chances. Be aware of standing water anywhere on or near your home, because it is a magnet for water bugs and mosquitos *(I also had a problem with mosquitos, now that I think about it. I guess that's three altercations.)*

Incident number two came upon returning home after a four-day weekend away. I opened the lidded trash can in my kitchen to find what appeared to be, upon first look, a bunch of white rice. That is until it started moving! Apparently, I had left food in the trash can and maggots were having a grand ol' time. After screaming myself hoarse, I replaced the lid (which was also covered on the underside), threw the entire bin in a large plastic trash bag, and brought it out to the curb. Vacation over. The lesson I learned was to always empty the trash before leaving for two nights or more. *Since then, I always have.*

The moral of the story is: prevention is key, quick response is best. Bugs happen regardless, so be prepared mentally if not always practically.

* * *

You Don't Need It

**ALWAYS BE THINKING OF HOW THINGS WORK…
AND HOW TO MAKE THE PROCESS EASIER**

Let's problem-solve. Maybe not everything has found a home, but you are almost completely unpacked and living in your space. You and your roommate have worked out your quirks and your icks and have gotten into a reasonable groove. Friends and family have come and gone, all loving the way you are standing on your own and making this place into a home. But it didn't go unnoticed when your parents came for lunch, they had to throw their coats over the couch. Or each time you head out to the laundromat, you always forget to take the detergent. Or when getting out of bed in the morning, you have to scoot down to the foot of the bed because the floor to the side of the headboard is blocked by your dresser, which you are also using as a nightstand. It's not a huge deal. You could certainly continue to live this way. But why? They may not be problems per se, but they are definitely irritants, the end of which are nothing more than a quick fix away.

As you use your space, give some thought to those moments where, in the midst of living/playing/working, you come across an "I wish I had X" case.

- Do you wish you had a coat closet? Hooks will work just as well. In fact, you can install them wherever a need to hang something has come up, since they are not just for coats. What about dish towels, your outfit for the next day, or your loofah in the shower? If you have a need to hang something somewhere, a hook will "hook you up."

- Are you always having to buy those pricey little boxes of detergent at the laundromat because you forget to bring yours with you? Why do you forget it? Is it not within eye shot when you grab your laundry basket or bag? Is it too heavy to carry? Divide it into portions using any plastic leftover containers and have them stacked in or near where you throw your laundry. Not only will it be easy to remember and carry, but you will always know when you are about to run out.

- As for having to scooch down your bed so you don't crack your head or knee on the corner of a piece of furniture taking up too much room, move it or replace it. Start by just trying to shift it a foot or so away from the bed. You may have to make adjustments to everything else in turn, but the momentary chore will be worth it to not conk your head when you roll over. If that doesn't work you may have to swap some things around. But as always, don't immediately buy a fix for the problem. See how you can work it out with what you have and then if all else fails, buy a true solution, not a temporary one.

You Don't Need It

RANT TIME: I need to rant about one of my all-time greatest pet peeves—clear plastic bins posing as two- and three-drawer furniture. You know the one I mean. They are usually sold in big box stores under the heading of "dorm essentials." They are ugly, they never work as intended, often coming out of the grooves or not closing all the way, and more importantly, you should never downgrade your life by purchasing what should only ever be given to you on a Buy Nothing level and used to hold kids' water toys in the backyard. Whew!

Now, as for a replacement piece next to your bed, I know you were being smart and using what you had on hand by going with that oversized piece of furniture. But sometimes, even with our best efforts, things don't work out as planned. *That's a lesson for life as well. Cut your losses and try something else.*

* * *

This chapter is about the act of living in your space. So far, we've talked about roommate communication for a more comfortable living environment, setting up your pantry for efficient use, and finding simple solutions for solving problems you didn't know you had until you had them. Now let's talk about maintenance and improvements.

MAINTAINING YOUR SPACE

Over or underestimating your motivation and physical energy can create massive hurdles to getting and keeping your space in order. I've run into this problem myself recently. As I write this, it is springtime, which means spring cleaning. Every year I attempt to do my "spring" cleaning in the winter because by the actual spring I want to be outside in my garden. I also figure, "What better time than when I'm stuck in the house anyway?" This year I did not have a plan. All I wrote on my calendar was "spring cleaning." As if that's all it took to get the job done. Well guess what? It didn't…get done, that is. And if I, someone for whom organizing is a passion hobby, procrastinates about spring cleaning, how can I expect you to do any better? Long story short, it's spring and only one floor of my three-story house has gotten the heavy duty clean this season usually brings with it.

Since most people take the term spring cleaning to mean "in the spring," many don't worry about it until then…if at all. And if they do choose to do this type of time and labor-intensive scrub, their issue is not about sleeping in on a grey, cold day instead of pulling out the ladder to wash the windows. No, in most cases, the issue that holds people back from a spring cleaning is "not planning" because it's all "too overwhelming." Here's my first piece of advice. DO NOT EVER make a to-do list that says something like "spring clean house" or even "spring clean bedroom". That's not nearly enough to get you started because frankly, that's not even a start.

"But Bonnie, why are we even talking about spring cleaning? I just moved in. I've got another year at least before I have to even consider doing this." Yes and no. Spring cleaning is a reset, pulling your home back to clutter-free, organized, sterile, ground zero. You have been living in your new space for just a few weeks or months and now you are in a position to correct mistakes with your clutter, furniture placement, habits, and chores before things get really out of hand. Then, when spring actually rolls around, no matter the mess you've let it devolve into, it won't be nearly as difficult to get it back on track.

So, here's spring cleaning in a nutshell. It is everything I've ever talked about, wrote about, and implored others to think about, all at once, in one massive event. One massive event that may take several days, weeks, or months, depending on how much time you have to invest or motivation you can muster. And it is totally worth it!

PROJECT: SPRING CLEANING PLANNING

- **Something to write with and something to write on.** *I suggest not using your phone or computer for this. When you're cleaning it can get messy. You don't want your electronics* *getting gunked up, or touch screens not working at all. Plus, a pen and paper are easier to shove in your pocket.*

Write down each room and each storage space, starting with the top floor, working your way down to the basement, then out to the garage/shed. *For example, in my house it would start something like this:*

- Bedroom
    - closet 1 (larger)
    - closet 2
    - dresser
    - storage trunks
    - downsize
    - remove decor
    - strip linens & wash
    - dust ceilings/ceiling fixtures
    - pull furniture out & clean
    - push furniture back & clean
    - wash windows
    - clean floors
    - assess your work & make revisions

- Hallway
    - hallway window seat storage
    - downsize
    - remove decor
    - dust ceilings/ceiling fixtures

- pull furniture out & clean
- push furniture back & clean
- wash windows
- clean floors
- assess your work & make revisions

- Bathroom
  - cabinet 1 (main)
  - cabinet 2
  - under sink
  - downsize
  - remove decor
  - strip towels & wash
  - dust ceilings/ceiling fixtures
  - heavy duty clean
  - wash windows
  - clean floors
  - assess your work & make revisions

- Bedroom
  - dresser
  - cubbies 1 (listed clockwise around room)
  - cubbies 2
  - cubbies 3
  - cubbies 4
  - downsize
  - remove decor
  - strip linens & wash
  - dust ceilings/ceiling fixtures
  - pull furniture out & clean

- push furniture back & clean
- wash windows
- clean floors
- assess your work & make revisions

Right about now you are losing the will to go on, and you're saying to yourself, "by the time I finish writing this damn list, it will be winter." But I promise, not only will this make the process more streamlined and faster, it will be incredibly motivating at the same time. Why? Because by doing things in this order, you will have less to clean. Let me continue.

Collect your supplies. Something for trash. Something for recycling. Something for castoffs (though don't try to figure out what you are doing with each piece just yet; it's enough to collect what you are getting rid of right now.) You will also need individual cleaning supplies and tools. Things like wood cleaner and rags, glass cleaner and paper towels, empty vacuum, filled wet vac, etc.

Dress appropriately. Hair out of your face. Closed-toe shoes. Work clothes you don't care about. And make sure you have eaten and have water on hand.

Make time. Clear your calendar of anything else for a few hours to make a serious dent in things. This is not the moment to tackle a project while you've got a few minutes.

PROJECT: SPRING CLEANING DOING

Go through all your storage areas. Sort. Downsize. I'm going to include an excerpt from chapter one of my first book, *STOP BUYING BINS*, because it best explains the process. This excerpt is specific to clothing, but it can be applied to anything that no longer serves you. Be thoughtful but don't overthink it. The goal overall is to have less to take care of. Period.

In an act of unwavering determination—and to end the constant dismay of having a crowded closet but never anything to wear—**I pulled it all out!** Everything! From every closet and drawer and shelf. From all over the house. Shoes and coats and pajamas and bridesmaid gowns. If I was going to do this I was going to do it right, and that meant all or nothing. There was no halfway in that moment for me. I was all in! I even threw in a **load of laundry** just so I wasn't missing anything. Now in front of me was every piece of clothing I owned with the exception of what I was wearing. And even that I wasn't so sure I would be keeping.

Eagerly facing the mound amassed high on my

bed, I started going through it item by item, **dividing everything into two simple piles—what fit and what did not**. Not what I wanted or needed or couldn't bear to part with. Not money spent, or memories attached, or the "but it's still good" refrain. NO, the only question was, **could I put it on my body?** And I didn't tell myself, "Oh, that fits," when I knew in my heart that getting it on and having it fit were two different things. This was an exercise in honesty with myself. There was no room for lying or pretending. This was going to be difficult and I was prepared for battle.

It started out pretty much as expected. Every piece that did not fit filled me with regret. The cocktail dress I wore to my cousin's wedding that I never had another reason to wear and now no longer could. That cropped sweater from college that I used to look so cute in that nowadays only accentuated my mommy midsection. The pants I got on sale that were never quite right to begin with but bought because I couldn't pass up that price. And with every piece I saw in my mind the money I'd spent. Some had tags, years old in fact, so I didn't even have to imagine. It was staring me right in the face. All the wasted money. All the wasted closet space. All the beating myself up for being too heavy to fit into the items of clothing that cost me money and took up space. All the regret for getting old and not living a life that kept me thin and gave me reason to wear those clothes that I wasted money on and that took up closet space. It's a deep, dark hole once you start digging down into the trench of regret. It seems easier to close the closet door and just keep wearing the clothes straight out of the laundry basket over and over. I know some of you reading this are really feeling me right now, and that it hurts. Deep breath, my friend. I understand and I'm here for you.

Regardless of the pain I was experiencing as the pile of "doesn't fit, won't fit, will never fit" was growing and toppling over onto the floor, I kept my goal in mind. Believe me, it wasn't all in strength, there were tears and a caffeine-fueled pity party or two. But nothing good comes from standing still. When it's hard, that's when you put your head down and keep going. Forging ahead, **I lumped together everything that did not fit and put it in another room.** Out of sight, out of mind. My ego was bruised, but I felt accomplished. And I rewarded myself with a quick 20-minute shuteye to regain my will to go on. Naps are the best!

Now back to what was in front of me. It was never more glaringly obvious that I was holding onto things that didn't serve me in any way than to see this sad, tiny assortment of make-do coordinates. Nearly 90% of what had been in my closet was now in another room, and it was time to get real with myself and **weed through the pile** in front of me. A pile of clothes that were too big and shapeless, or hung funny off my curvier parts, or were faded, pilling, or just plain ugly. There were so many mornings when I'd walk into my closet and just put on anything regardless of its attractiveness or how it made me feel to wear it. They were clothes just to cover my body. And now, faced with what I had truly been wearing for years, I had to admit I hated most of it. So I did what I had to do. **I added them to the "out" pile** in the other room.

What was left, I rehung. For a full week after, I didn't touch the pile in the other room. I didn't even look at it. Instead, every morning that week, I walked into what was now my essentially vacant closet and no matter what I put on, it fit, looked good, and made me just the slightest bit confident. No longer was I burdened by those "one day" or "can't part with them" clothes. I didn't have to try on endless items to find something comfortable, nor did I have to rehang everything that I tried on but didn't work. I didn't have to turn away from all the regret-provoking clothes to home in on the few useful pieces I had. And even though there was very little left, I was immediately surprised to find myself enjoying getting dressed each day. No more feelings of failure. I breathed easier, I held my posture better, I smiled more. Why? I hadn't lost weight or bought anything new. All I did was free myself from the self-inflicted punishment of stuff in my closet that no longer served any positive purpose. So what's next, you ask? What did I do with the clothes in the other room? Well, that part is easy.

Gift.
Donate.

Sell.

After that week had gone by and I hadn't missed any of it, I knew it all had to go. **Some went to friends** (the cocktail dress), **the bulk went to charity** (the cropped sweater), **a few pieces I held back to sell** (the pants that still had tags). But all of it was gone a few days later. And it was freeing! Did I have any regrets? Yes and no. I regretted making the mistake of keeping those things in the first place more than I ever did in giving them away. I didn't miss them at all. Why would I? I wasn't wearing them. Some I hadn't worn in decades. What then was I really missing? And that empty closet? It was looking like something staged for an organizing segment on morning TV where each piece hangs freely on its own barely touching the one next to it, all in color spectrum harmony.

* * *

Let me bottomline this for those of you just waiting for me to get to the bullet points. Don't start this project unless you can **devote the time to getting it done in one go around**, otherwise all you will have accomplished is pulling your mess out into the light of day and eventually having to sleep on it.

1. **Do the laundry.** You're going to want all your clothes in front of you for this project. That

includes the week's worth of dirty socks in the hamper that in all honesty should just be thrown out because of the holes in the heels.

2. **Pull everything out of the closets and drawers from all over the house.** This includes everything from the ski jacket with the 30-year-old lift ticket on the zipper stored in the attic to the slippers from under your bed that are fuzzy with dust bunnies. Pants and activewear and even undergarments get pulled out. You should be looking at everything.

ADVICE: Speaking of underthings, an ill-fitting bra changes everything from how your clothes hang on you to your overall posture. Several years ago, I started going to a bra shop where I was fitted by a professional. I found that the bras were not any more expensive than the ones I had previously bought in department stores and in the long run, far cheaper than the cheap bras that never fit right. It's well worth it and can ultimately be life changing. Nothing else matters but proper fit. Get rid of anything that doesn't.

3. **Separate your clothes into two piles.** There is only one question to ask yourself: "Does it fit?" Not "Could it fit?" or "Will it fit?" "<u>Does it fit?" Full stop!</u> I know you're saying, "But those are still good!" Well, yes, they are. But not for you. Don't bog yourself down with the

value—monetary or emotional. For now, you just want a pile of clothes that you can wear and a pile that you can't.

4. **Take the out pile and put it in another room.** This is an experiment—out of sight, out of mind. They are not part of what you are doing now. Don't waste a moment thinking about them or what you might eventually do with them.

5. **Break down the "does fit" pile.** There are a few more questions to ask yourself. Does it fit well? Is it attractive on? Is it in good condition? Do you still like it? Do you have any use for it? Answer NO to any of these questions and it gets added to the out pile. Keep only the items where the answer is YES to all questions.

6. **Everything that is a YES gets put neatly back in your closet and drawers.** Live out of your new collection of clothes for a week. **Wear them in rotation.** If there is anything that you consistently pass over, chances are you are not going to wear that either. Out it goes. "But if I get rid of everything, I'll have nothing to wear!" Guess what—you already had nothing to wear. What's left is all you were actually wearing anyway.

7. Now for the **pile in the other room.** Remind yourself that NOTHING is coming back into your space! NOTHING! Instead **determine ways to give all these things a new life.**
    → Have your friends over and let them just take what they want.
    → Have a yard sale and put the money away for your next shopping trip.
    → Take the winter weather items to a shelter.
    → Sell them through a consignment shop.
    → Donate the whole lot to a charity of your choice—most even take items that are stained or worn and recycle them.
    → None of it needs to be thrown away. Likewise, none of it is a part of your life anymore.

Whew! How do you feel? Better than you thought you would, admit it. You want to know why? Aside from the obvious mental and physical clutter overload that these excess pieces of clothing were creating, they were also wreaking havoc with your self-esteem. I know all too well those feelings of failure when you are desperately trying to find something to wear and nothing fits, trying on piece after piece that is too tight or makes you look like a blob, playing out scenarios in your head about how people will think you've let yourself go. That feeling of self-consciousness and awkwardness, sucking in any body part you can, trying to gloss over your insecurities with banter so no one notices what you look like. (Can you tell I have anxiety issues?) It's exhausting! And depressing. And the worst possible way to motivate anyone to get fit and thin. Incentive clothes DO NOT WORK! Although they do kinda make me want to run… toward a bowl of pasta.

Once you've done the work, your space and head will be free and clear. No need to feel defeated for gaining weight or living in clutter. You've seen the error of your ways and realize you don't have to live with those fashion failures as a constant, guilt-inducing reminder. Nor will you have to hunt through a mountain of closet chaos to find what fits. It's in that joy that you will be motivated to lose weight, if you so wish to be motivated. You are living in the now, where your dresser drawers open and close smoothly because they are not filled with balled-up clothes preventing them from working properly. And the closet, with the floor you hadn't seen in years because of clutter, is now a place filled with clothes that feel custom made for you. What a rush!

Now that you no doubt have a lot less clothes, don't make the mistake of filling your space back up after you've done the hard work of paring down. Don't just go out and shop. Think about what you are really missing, what you really need, what would make you happy to own, and then by all means, go and find it. But don't bring home any "maybe this will work" or "this is good enough" or "it's not quite right but it's on sale" pieces.

If you can't find exactly what you're looking for, keep looking. And if you don't need anything, enjoy the space. There is always the option of just living with less.

ADVICE: Do you feel like shopping for a few new seasonal items to spruce up your look but don't want to mess with the perfection of your newly streamlined dream closet? **Give to get!** Collect a bag of castoffs, and drop them at the donation center on your way to the shops. Ideally, one piece out for one piece in, but if you want to be really brave, two for one is the best way to go. It's that easy!

"But wait," you say. "Fit is not my issue. I'm the same size I was in high school." First, I'd reply "Wow, good for you," in as sarcastic a tone as I could muster, followed by a wink and a laugh to let you know I'm just kidding around, and then go on to explain that **this system works the same way for any of your overcrowded wardrobe woes.** Do you have several lifetimes sharing space in your closet? Do you have an abundance of impulse purchases? Do you have drawers of T-shirts from every concert you've ever attended that have more holes than fabric? Or do you just have too much because it's "still good"? I think you know what I'm going to suggest. Purge, purge, and purge some more. At one point I owned more yoga pants than someone who has never actually taken a yoga class before should own. I pared them down to a single-digit collection by returning anything still tagged. Yes, I might eventually use them, but why have my money tied up in spandex when I already had nine pairs in rotation? I wish that were a joke but it's not, so feel free to laugh.

Here are the questions to ask yourself if you just have more clothes than space:

- **Is it in any way damaged—stained, faded, missing fasteners, misshapen by wash, etc.?**
- **Does it look good on you?**
- **Do you wear it regularly?**
- **Have you worn it recently?**
- **Is it still tagged after months in your closet?**
- **Do you honestly have any use for it?**
- **Would someone you know get better use out of it?**
- **Did you wear it but no longer need it?**
- **Did you buy it on sale because it was on sale?**
- **Did you forget you had it?**
- **Do you still like it?**
- **Have you read through all of these questions and still are saying "but it's still good"?**

You know what I'm going to say now. If you're not using it, move it along. But hey, this is a book about downsizing clutter. If you have a mansion-sized celebrity closet with a strobe light runway, keep it all! You've got the room. If not, something, excuse me, a lot of things, have to go!

Last point I'd like to reiterate. You've pulled it all out. You've asked yourself the right questions. You've made your piles and sent a good percentage of clothes onto their next adventure. Now you're starting each day with this renewed wardrobe. But you still somehow keep bypassing that yellow button down shirt. It fits, you have reason to wear it, and it's in good condition. But it's not in the rotation. **Either work it onto the team roster or make it a free agent.** We're not keeping things for no good reason anymore. Use it or lose it.

Bottom line, these are clothes. Most of us don't have bespoke designer Met Gala–worthy duds made of archival silk spun by magic fairies. Our clothes came from a store off a rack with thousands of other identical pieces. Letting go of them is not all that difficult precisely for that reason—they are replaceable. What cannot be replaced, however, are physical space in your home, time spent getting dressed, self-respect when you feel unattractive or defeated, and money lost on useless purchases. Please take that all into consideration the next time you say, "But I can't get rid of it" and then promptly return it to the back of the closet with the other clothes you haven't worn in years.

Nothing is more important when it comes to your clothes, or your life for that matter, than feeling comfortable and confident with yourself. Don't punish yourself for growing old, gaining weight, making impulse purchases, or holding onto things past their point of usefulness. Instead, let go of the triggering item, absolve yourself of the error in judgment, and give yourself permission to be who you are now in this moment. I for one am happy to say that after that overhaul, my wardrobe is filled only with clothes perfectly suited to me. Should the need arise for something new, I vow to buy only what fits, is appropriate for the occasion, and makes me look and feel fantastic. Fingers crossed it's also on sale.

~~~~~~~~~~~~~~~~~~~~~~~~~~~~~~

Does that help explain the downsizing process a bit better? And with that complete, it's time to take a break. That was a lot! You've earned it. But if you are still motivated and want to keep going, let's do it!

- **Remove all decor items including lamps, electronics, and wall art.** *Collect these items and put them outside the room. We will get back to them later.*

- **Strip the bed of all bedding and wash. Cover the mattress with a flat sheet for the next step.**

- **Run a long duster across the ceiling, and ceiling lights and fans, to collect dust or cobwebs. (And yes, you have both.)** *Don't worry about dust* *falling on furniture. You will be cleaning them next. As for the mattress, that is what the sheet in the last step is for.*

- **Pull all furniture away from walls.** *You might want to wear a mask for this. Even after just a few months of living in your place, there WILL be dust. Possibly lots of it. Dust the backs of furniture, dust and vacuum the walls and floors behind furniture, and pay attention to the electric outlets, which are magnets for "dust bunnies".*

- **Push the furniture back and complete the furniture-cleaning process using the appropriate cleaners. Don't forget the floors underneath. And to vacuum all parts of the bed, from the rails to the mattress.** *This is also the time to reassess moving furniture around for better flow and function. Oh, and flip the mattress too!*

- **Grab a ladder and wash the windows.** *This includes removing the screens and vacuuming them. Assess them for damage and make repairs, especially if you are going to be letting the fresh air in this spring. You don't want to also be letting in bugs. Oops! I almost forgot to tell you, wash or at least dust the doors, front and back. Door knobs are grime attractors.*

- **Clean your decor.** *Dust it. Wash it. Get rid of it. This is your opportunity to redecorate your space* *by "shopping your stuff." You are by no means obligated to put it all back.*

- **Finally, vacuum or wet dust the floors.** *As you navigate the room with your equipment, are you able to get into all areas easily? Are there areas that are going to be consistently missed in your regular cleaning? There are two options here. Either make a change now so these spaces are accessible, or make a mental note to special clean those areas from time to time. This very much includes under the bed. AND, it helps if you never store anything under your bed. MAJOR PET PEEVE OF MINE!*

- **Before you are completely done, consider if something works better somewhere else.** Take the time to think through the placement of furniture by considering how you will use it and what makes the most sense for the items. That makeshift bar area and mini fridge stocked with White Claw look great by the window, but direct sunlight on your wine rack is not ideal for the wine. Putting them closer to the cabinet where you will keep the glasses, on the other hand, eliminates moving them when you entertain since they will already be nearby. Practicality always trumps pretty, but it's not an either/or proposition; you can have both. The upside to putting practicality first is that it makes it easier to keep it pretty.

- **Stand back and take a look at your work.** *How do you feel? Hopefully happy. Hopefully accomplished. Because if you did in fact do all the work outlined, you deserve a break, a treat, and "Good Job!"*

Now go through your other rooms and spaces, and do the same. Start with a list you can check off as you go. I LOVE CHECKMARKS! Downsize, clean it all, put it back together better than before. It's that easy! Hahaha.

TOTAL COST: FREE (if you have all the supplies already); you may even make some money if you sell the items you downsize.

* * *

STORY TIME FROM BEFORE YOUR TIME

Whatever your definition of clean may be, know where on the spectrum of acceptable practices you lie. My house is almost always organized, habitually neat, generally clean, rarely chaotic. *I may have spoken too soon. I think I have dishes in the sink right now.* By the standards of most, anyone can stop by my home and feel comfortable. They haven't caught my house on an off day *(me, not so much.)* But I have been in homes… wait, let me rephrase, I have been invited to homes, for special events, with multiple guests *(just so you know*

I didn't just pop-in) that were downright filthy. And I'm not talking about accidentally spilled pasta salad on the floor during the party prep. I'm talking about caked on crud that hasn't been cleaned since it first came to be stuck there. Which suggests the area as a whole has not been cleaned. Probably ever.

"So where is the story, Bonnie?" OK, so there is not a specific story because there are too many stories of homes I have been in as an invited guest, not as an organizer or decorator, that have made my skin crawl. Where sitting on a seat meant either asking for a sponge to clean it off first or just sitting in the crumbs and spills and pet hair, and dealing with my clothes when I got home by stripping down inside the front door.

I'm not suggesting your home always be spotless—well, actually I would love that—only that you never let your home get to the point where tossing a lit match and walking away is the only option. **Keep your home neat and clean and clutter free. Show it respect. The respect you have for your home is a reflection of the respect you have for yourself, and you deserve a high level of respect.**

Or, if your house is a biohazard, don't invite people over.

6

Decorate With Restraint

It seems like there are endless rules when it comes to decorating, on top of which it's nearly impossible to follow them all, since they come from all different designers and often contradict each other. Let's take, for example, two powerhouse style icons whose personal fashion extended to their interiors. The epitome of refinement, Coco Chanel is famously quoted as saying, "Before you leave the house, look in the mirror and take at least one thing off." While Iris Apfel, no doubt wearing her maximalist signature look said, "More is more and less is a bore." So how exactly is anyone supposed to know how to decorate their homes? **As far as I'm concerned, there are only three rules:**

1. **Don't have anything in your home you don't love.**

2. **Don't have more than you can maintain.**
3. **Don't do it all at once…decorating is a lifelong journey.**

These three rules can be applied to any style of décor, from 1700s Rococo to1970s rec room. But where to start? Start with that vision board you created for yourself way back at the start of this book. Pull it out, dust it off, and see where you stand now. Do you still see yourself in those photos, or has the process of planning and moving and problem-solving changed your perspective? Maybe a gallery wall no longer appeals to you because dusting it weekly is not something you anticipated and it's now a dealbreaker. Maybe the same goes for the tweed throw pillows your roommate's cat loves to use as a scratching post. Or maybe you are just realizing, as beautiful as those pictures you collected are, you just can't accomplish that look on your salary. You know what I'm going to say to that last one…reread the chapter titled "Find Free Before Financing."

I've touched on all these "rules" in other chapters and in other books. *They wouldn't be rules if I didn't live by them.* But I'm going to break each one down and give real world examples to better clarify why I've made them my only three. Here goes.

RULE ONE: DON'T HAVE ANYTHING IN YOUR HOME YOU DON'T LOVE.

"Bonnie, why would I have anything in my home I don't love? That's obvious." Is it though? You know you've got some tchotchke your aunt gave you as a housewarming gift. Maybe a little square wood cube that reads "Dance like nobody's watching." You get her intent (you used to take ballet as a kid) and you appreciate the thoughtfulness in her giving you a gift, but it doesn't quite give off the same vibe as your dark academia aesthetic…even if it does have words on it. So tell me, do you love it?

What *do* you love? Whatever it is, decorating with it is as simple as gathering it all together, assessing what you have, curating, editing, and deciding how to display it. Don't complicate it for yourself. The common thread doesn't have to be much more than a color or a shape. Let me give you an example.

I love the color green! Green leaning towards blue, not yellow. I'm kind of obsessed with it. Nearly every shade and variation on that end of the color wheel will do. I will choose almost any item over another based solely on this color. As a result, green plays a huge part in my interior space. From table linens and bed linens to wall art and wall paint, if it's green, I'm drawn to it. So can an entire aesthetic be based solely on a color? Why not? Color does make a compelling commonality among objects. It ties everything together in a neat green bow. Especially when it extends beyond the color to the meaning—think "going green." Potted plants, reclaimed wood, upcycled used furniture, repurposed thrift store finds—a seeming hodgepodge of random items that sing harmoniously together. And it all starts with a color.

So, what do you think? Do you have something you love and can build on? Is there a certain color, design, hobby, or lifestyle that gives you a feeling of utter bliss? Lean in and make it your own. And there are so many ways to achieve it. You could take what you have and craft a common denominator, if there isn't one already. You could go on a thrifting trip and curate "new to you" finds from store to store. You could go to IKEA and buy every item with the same unpronounceable name. *But you already know what I'm going to say about that last one.* Let's do a project!

PROJECT: COLLECTION CURATION
- all your stuff to decorate with
- a few empty boxes for downsizing (gift, sell, donate)
- a surface to work from

This is going to be fun, I promise. Not only because you will get an opportunity to enjoy your collection, but you will exercise your curating muscle by having all your things in one place to compare to each other. What do I mean? When one piece stands alone, you might think it's a must-keep. But when it's amongst other items, you may feel it's just not as good or important an item as you previously thought. Or it just doesn't go with the others. This might seem like a lengthy process, but honestly it's minutes, if that long.

1. You've gathered together your favorite things. Now separate them into like items, let's say Pokémon stuff and cat figurines. *Hey, no judgement, just proving it can be anything.*

2. Of those groupings, do all the items in each group seem to "go" together, or are they random? Meaning, are the cats all the same size or material or style, or are they varied in a way that doesn't mesh? It's completely up to you what that means. I might not want to put a plastic charm kitten with a word bubble that says "Meow" next to a bone china replica of an Egyptian Sphynx cat, but you certainly could. *(Though to be honest, I'd take the charm over the replica; those cats creep me out.)*

3. Once you've separated each grouping further, some more decisions can be made. Does one grouping look sparse by comparison? Do you have duplicates? Do you need both? Is anything here worthy of being displayed on its own, or is it more of a

lump-it-together-in-a-decorative-container situation? Do you really love them, or are you just trying to pull things together to decorate with?

4. Likewise, once you've separated them, do you think you need MORE? *Such a loaded question coming from me. We'll just put that one aside for the moment.*

PROJECT WITHIN A PROJECT: Take all the little plastic doodads that are too small to display on their own and **put them all in a lidded jar.** Label or decorate the lid and **use it as a bookend or a doorstop.** Now you've both contained them and made them useful, plus with a lid, dust free.

Addressing that earlier question of "do you think you need MORE?" the answer is *no*. And also, *maybe*. Decorate with the items you have and leave it at that for the moment. Decorating is a lifelong endeavor. You're going to be in situations throughout your life to find those can't-live-without pieces that catch your eye, and you're not going to want to say to yourself, "Oh, I can't buy this magical piece of pottery while I'm in Japan because I already have too much mass-produced crap from Pottery Barn." *If that sounds like me, it is, but only because I DID buy the magical Japanese pottery because I don't own anything from Pottery Barn.* NOW, let's finish up the project we started.

5. Take your groupings and display them. *Wait! What?! Is that it? That's all you're going to say?* Haha! Sort of. I'm not going to tell you where to put them or how, but rather, like at other moments in this book, I will give you **things to consider before you place these items.**

   a. Will you, for example, be covering the entire surface of the table with items, or will you still be using the surface area? Your collection of items should not have to be moved every time you use the space. Keep your display area controlled—the center of a table, or the far front of a desk.

   b. Are your items delicate or intricate? Consider grouping them under glass to keep them safe and dust free—cloches, bell jars, and cake domes work exceptionally well.

   c. Are your items top-heavy or wobbly? Don't place them anywhere where they might be knocked over, or where even the foot traffic passing them will cause them to teeter.

   d. Will you be accessing this display, or items housed around the display, on a regular basis? Make sure those items you need regularly are easily accessible and your displays are not in the way or at risk of being damaged. *(Maybe don't place your Fabergé egg on your bathroom counter next to your toothbrush. Haha.)*

e. Groupings of items do have a general rule you can follow if you so choose. They are: 1 large item alone, 2 same size pairs, 3 of graduated sizes, or any more items than that go larger/taller in the back and smaller in the front or larger/taller in the center and smaller around. Playing with it until you're happy with how it looks is really the only way.

TOTAL COST: FREE
(until that must-have item crosses your path)

SIDE STORY: Working with clients as an interior decorator wasn't always easy for me. My skills lie in problem solving, seeing where something can be improved and tweaked, not necessarily making things pretty for pretty's sake. I've always been better at moving furniture around for better flow, choosing a wall covering to highlight a favorite piece of furniture or upholstery, or editing knickknacks (i.e., decluttering). And unlike organizing, which can be explained in simple-to-follow lists, decorating is individual and personal, and tapping into the mindset of a client and immediately understanding their tastes is a herculean task. After a few fumbles, I changed my approach to decorating for clients by telling them I'd be happy to help use what they already have, suggest something I thought they could use, upcycle existing pieces by reupholstering or painting, hire contractors to do any work, and/or guide them through the process of doing it for themselves, BUT that I prefer not to create a room from scratch. I'm not sure now if that had more to do with being scared to impose my vision on them or just that I like the aspects of reclaiming and repurposing, but as a business model it was a success! Not only could they take ownership of the project and inject their own vision into it, but also it was significantly cheaper for them to pay for my advice than for a roomful of new designer furnishings and decor that they had no real attachment to.

* * *

Let's stay on the subject of "more" for a moment. If furniture is the cake and home decor is the cake decoration, then when is there too much icing?

Or too little?

Or, what size and scale will work?

Should they be useful or merely decorative?

Should they be personal or just pretty?

Original or mass produced?

You Don't Need It

Bold or subtle?

Expensive or cheap?

Will this list ever end or will I keep going?

I already said it. There are only three rules. And remember, the first one is **don't have anything in your home that you don't love. And if you love it, it doesn't matter if you are breaking some arbitrary rule.** You will know when something doesn't work. It will feel off (out of place with everything else), or obvious (drawing undeserved attention to itself), or contrived (not natural and overly staged.) Also, it doesn't matter where you got the item, how much it cost, or whether it serves any purpose. The only thing that matters, after loving it, is…

RULE TWO: DON'T HAVE MORE THAN YOU CAN MAINTAIN.

Books, clothes, or even handmade pottery—if you have too much, you can't possibly maintain it all. And by that, I mean keep it clean, keep it in good repair, and keep it orderly. If you have clothes thrown on a chair next to your closet and you've been telling yourself you just have to "organize" it, but the reason it is not organized is that you can't shove another hanger on the rod, then it looks like you're going to have to get rid of some clothes. Same for those piles of books on every available surface where you might read them because your bookshelves are full. Even my beloved pottery collection has reached maximum capacity. **If I find something new that I can't live without, that means something I currently own has to go. It's that simple…and that difficult.**

But limited square footage is just one reason for keeping your inventory low. There is also the keeping it clean part. Dust is not your friend. I know that there are dust-sucking air purifying units available, but that doesn't solve the problem of having too many things to dust. And I say "dust," but that is just one of the conditions that prompt you to have to clean. There is also pet fur and dander, cooking grease, cobwebs, and actual dirt, to name a few.

The more you have, the more you will have to clean, and the more time it will take to do that cleaning. And what "fresh out of college, working at their first big city job" young adult (should that be your path) wants to spend any time cleaning? Er, none. So bear that in mind before you take up every table surface, nook, and wall molding with Marvel figurines and your favorite professional sports team memorabilia. No one's got that kind of time.

RULE THREE: DON'T DO IT ALL AT ONCE… DECORATING IS A LIFELONG JOURNEY

I've mentioned before *(yes, I have a habit of repeating myself)* that your home is a never-ending evolution… just like you. You will acquire, you will be given, you will make, you find in your travels all sorts of items that will tell the story of your life, and you will likely display them proudly in your home as a reminder of a life well lived. Generally speaking, you are not going to accumulate all those items at once, then set it and forget it. Nor are they likely to come from buying the complete setup on page 42 of the IKEA catalog including every Finiss and Fyrkantig *(you can look them up; they're real).* That's why I implore you to use what you have, maybe even edit down your stock, and not rush to fill every space right away. There will be time enough for that.

SIDE STORY: For all my talk of paring down and leaving space, I myself can be classified as a maximalist. Some *(mostly those people that have read my books and found my tone to be judgmental)* would probably call me a hypocrite, but how I decorate is for me, and I follow all three of my own rules. I love it! I maintain it! And I acquire it over time! Martha Stewart calls our mutual love of stuff "clustercore" (others call it "cluttercore"), but I have also heard it referred to as "organized clutter" or "intentional clutter."

What it boils down to is that I like to be surrounded by stuff that makes me happy. It's not broken or dirty, it's not piled on top of each other in a corner, it's not packed in a box shoved to the back of a closet or garage. It is out where I can see it and enjoy it and use it daily. And if there is more than you think is a

Decorate With Restraint

reasonable amount, I say to you, good thing you don't live here. See, I'm not telling you how to live. I'm giving you guidelines on how to live, in any way you want to live, to the fullest.

"Bonnie, you keep talking about all this stuff I'm supposedly moving into my first apartment. But all I've got is a mattress and a coffee table. That's all I need." Well then, as long as you love the way you live, that's all that matters. Minimalism is a beautiful lifestyle. So while we're on the subject, let's talk about minimalism, because it's more than just living sparsely.

Minimalism is intentional. And that mattress and coffee table would be meticulously kept and preserved as a result of intentionality. You would treasure the items around you so they continue to serve you. Your life would be spent mostly in the pursuit of art and culture and nature, which would serve as all the adornment you would need to bring you happiness.

However, if this living arrangement comes out of need or want (of money, interest, direction) then you are not living like a minimalist. You might be living with a mindset of lack. "Oh, I don't have the money to have nice things, so what's the point of trying to make my house nice?" Because it doesn't take money, as I've said umpteen times! You can live a beautiful life! You can live in a beautiful home! It can restore and rejuvenate you mentally, physically, and spiritually... or it can make you feel sad and drained. And those negative emotions can be attributed to either clutter or to dearth. Find a happy medium by *(dare I say it again)* only having what you love or need, and only what you can take care of. A home where everywhere your eye lands holds something that makes you smile is pure bliss. Achievable, attainable, it's-yours-for-the-taking bliss.

It doesn't have to cost you a lot of money. And it doesn't have to be done immediately. And it doesn't take much more than leaning into who you are. I'm going to tell you something. If you say you don't care about decorating, I'm going to reply, you only think you don't care about decorating. You may think you don't have any interest in style, but do you have another particular interest? Do you, for example, enjoy listening to music? Lying on a comfy couch in a beam of sunlight, headphones on, eyes closed, listening to your music of choice, maybe even on vinyl? There you go! That's how you're going to decorate at least that area, if not your whole place. Do you have a green thumb? Plant it up! A fondness for frogs? Hop on over to the internet where you will find at least a dozen easy-to-install, easy-to-remove peel-and-stick wallpapers with your favorite amphibians on them. Still think decorating is not for you? It is, as long as you do it for you!

* * *

Decorate With Restraint

STORY TIME FROM BEFORE YOUR TIME

My former husband and I had received two round-trip airline tickets to anywhere in the US as a wedding gift. Wanting to take advantage of this rare opportunity, we threw a dart at a map and went to Santa Fe, New Mexico. It was an incredible experience, still etched in my memory from 30 years ago.

It was on that trip that I purchased my first pieces of handmade pottery—four pots/vases and a dozen hand-painted tiles *(which caused quite a stir coming through security because of the way they were wrapped like dense black boxes.)* At the time I bought them, they were more a reminder of the trip. Over the years, as I rearranged items in my houses to accommodate the comings and goings of things, two pieces *(both green, which I mentioned before is my fav)* rose to the rank of favorites, always finding their way into places of prominence. Then I began to add others to the family, blending shades of green and then blue, until I had more than I could comfortably keep. I have purchased, been gifted, repurposed, broken, donated, sold, found, given away, sorted, edited, and even made so much pottery in the last three decades I've lost count. It brings me so much joy! I keep my collection to an amount that doesn't look cluttered to me, and more importantly, doesn't take long to dust. And I have absolutely no intention of stopping!

Part 3:

FOREVER AFTER

7

"Use It Up, Wear It Out, Make It Do, or Do Without"

I don't know where I heard this saying first. I know my mother used to say it. Though more than likely, it came from my grandmother, who lived during the depression. It feels right to me because it speaks to a Yankee sensibility I've always possessed, even though I only just recently moved to New England. Regardless of whether I bought a new or previously owned car, I was the last person to drive it because I "used it up." Same with clothes, either straight from the department store or bought secondhand, that have been "worn out" to the point they can no longer be repaired. In the case of home decor, why have custom window treatments made when you can hang a flat sheet from some curtain hooks on a tension bar and "make it work?" Or, as is the case in my new house, just "do without" window treatments all together because I love the natural light.

If you'd like to incorporate this philosophy into your life, what is the best way to begin? **Don't buy another thing until what you have is completely used up.**

USE IT UP

There are two new year resolution ideas making the rounds on social media. As the name suggests, "No Buy" is just that—putting a halt on all new unnecessary purchases. Similarly, "Project Pan"—i.e., using your products up to the bottom of the "pan" or container—suggests not buying any new consumable products until you have completely used up what you have.

PROJECT: NO BUY
- **Decide immediately to not make any purchases of nonessentials**—clothes, home decor, furnishings, entertainment, eating out, etc.
- **End all subscriptions or memberships** that you do not use regularly, or negotiate a lower price for those you do use.
- **Only make purchases when absolutely needed.**
- **Find cheaper or free options for what you would typically spend on.**

For fun, keep a running total of what you spend for the month and try to spend less the following month. If you continue, you can see the results

"Use It Up, Wear It Out, Make It Do, or Do Without"

year over year and put the difference towards a larger purchase or experience.

PROJECT: PROJECT PAN

- **Make a list of all your everyday supplies,** from your toothpaste to your tomato sauce—everything you buy on a regular basis.
- **Gather those items together,** from what you are currently using to the extras you have stored away somewhere.
- **Decide if what you have is of use to you.** I know there have been moments in my life where there was a bottle of shampoo in my linen closet I bought, used once, and didn't like. If you have no intentions of using it, get rid of it. That doesn't mean throwing it out. There are several avenues to donate or give away these products.
- Now, **don't buy any more until you absolutely need it.** Does that feel uncomfortable? Yup. It will be until you get used to it. You know what is also uncomfortable? Having cash tied up in a backstock of body wash when you want to go out to dinner with friends.
- **Consider before restocking** if this is truly meeting your needs or if a change is in order. You will always need toilet paper, but maybe you don't need the three-ply, super fluffy

brand, or the 48-roll pack you were using as a side table because you had nowhere to store it.
- **Keep a list of things nearing their end.** Once you begin to use the last of any product, write it on your shopping list for the next time you buy supplies. But you have time, so don't rush. And remember, you only really need one to use and one as backup. The fact is, as comforting as it is to have lots of supplies on hand, buying in bulk is only ever necessary when there is a significant cost benefit, you go through supplies quickly, or you live out of reach of a store. Most of you will live in an area where you will pass a grocery store on a regular basis and can always stop for a quick pick-up if need be.

SIDE STORY: For nearly the last three decades, I have lived out of my home state of New Jersey. Every Christmas before heading back to visit family, we have a tradition I call **"Eating Down the Kitchen."** No fancy Christmas Eve meal for us unless you mean the smorgasbord of leftovers and sandwich makings all pulled out and reheated so nothing is left going bad in the fridge while we are away. And as a side bonus, we can start the new year with a newly stocked supply once we get back.

In recent years I've taken this a step further as a way of saving money and extending the time between grocery store visits. I have gone so far as to have nothing left but open condiments. I've even dumped them too because sometimes you don't know you hate something until you open a jar, try it, and then without thinking, just add it to the shelves on the refrigerator door, where it stays unopened for the next several months. In any event, it's a quirky way to clear things out in order to clean and start fresh—fuzzy olive tapenade and all. Plus, and as importantly, **it stretches your food budget. And who starting out living on their own can't benefit from that?**

WEAR IT OUT

I live my life in "wear it out" mode. From clothes to cars, I consider it a badge of honor to have owned, repaired, kept it in good condition, patched back together, and loved whatever it is immensely in the process. Trying to keep something working for as long as possible by repairing it, and then possibly giving it a second life by repurposing it, not only **extends that product's usefulness, but also saves money and the planet.**

NOTE: BUT DO NOT…hold onto anything by saying to yourself, "I'll use it for something" and then never do. Better to donate it for someone else to reuse in their own way, than keep it for the possibility of maybe one day putting it to use. **That's a fast car to hoarding, and it's a non-starter here! Don't do it!**

I love the fact that there is a rise in people mending worn clothes instead of just tossing them away. If you still love it, why not make repairs so you can continue to wear it, right? I also love the idea of upcycling secondhand clothes. Not only tailoring clothes to fit you better, but taking more than one piece to build something completely new and unique. Think quilts into coats, or dress shirts into decorative pillows. It can be anything your imagination (and a needle and thread) can dream up.

SIDE STORY: My grandmother was a dressmaker. Her first job was at Bergdorf Goodman, altering and tailoring dresses for the wealthy women of New York City. She offered me ample opportunities to learn how to sew. I got as far as learning how to run thread through the machine and making a bobbin, both skills I have long since lost. Not knowing how to sew, and more importantly, not learning this from her, is one of my biggest regrets. If you ever get the opportunity to learn a new skill, especially from a professional, take it.

Wearing out your clothes gives them that feeling of being well loved. Unfortunately the same cannot be said of furnishings or home decor, which when worn look more abused than cherished. Extending the longevity and usefulness of our surroundings comes down to taking care of our things and making repairs or improvements when necessary. I'm not even talking

"Use It Up, Wear It Out, Make It Do, or Do Without"

about altering or upcycling, which is of course an ideal path to prevent discarding your old items. I'm suggesting something far more practical—maintenance. Maintenance is how you keep something working for you until you have exhausted all it has to give. Until you have worn it out. From your favorite chair that has lost all its padding to the body-shaped cavern in your mattress, maintenance will keep these items working for you until they must be replaced.

With that in mind, **here are some quick home maintenance tasks to put on your calendar.** There are hundreds, but I'm going to give you my top five. Take what works for you, disregard the others, add your own. Build on them over time. These practices will save you so much money and many headaches in the long run. And here's another quick bit of advice: YouTube is your friend. If you don't know how to do something, someone in the world has made a video showing you exactly how to do it. OK. Let's jump into the list.

- Flip your mattress over from the long side at the six month mark. Then spin your mattress from top to bottom six months later. Continue switching these tasks every six months. What this does is compress the coils or foam, depending on the type of mattress you have, in both directions. The first time, you'll switch from one sleeping surface to the other, and if you sleep with a partner, you will also be changing what side of the mattress you are lying on without having to actually change the side of the bed you sleep on. The second time, you will be switching from your head to your feet and again, if you sleep with a partner, you will be going back to your original side, but on the flipside of the mattress. It's confusing to write it out without showing you, but if you are having trouble understanding, that's where YouTube comes in. This simple practice can keep your mattress in good shape for years, even decades if it's a good quality mattress. BONUS: take the time to fully vacuum the mattress, bed frame, headboard, bed rails, footboard, and under the bed each time. Dust is at its worst in and around your bed.

- Trim all loose threads on anything fabric. Pulling them could result in snagging or ripping the fabric. Leaving them just looks messy. Throwing them in the wash that way results in a tangled mess. It's an easy fix, so build the habit. I keep scissors on every level of my house so they are readily available to snip a string.

- Wash your washing machine…and dishwasher and garbage disposal, because they will get gunked up. Cleaning them regularly will prevent poor performance, abate odor, and keep repairs to a minimum. And do it even if you are a renter *(who wants some service person in your house while you're at work?)* There are easy baking soda and white vinegar hacks for these appliances (YouTube) but the cleaning tabs you can buy are relatively cheap, so that is also an option. The biggest cause of issues in these areas are trapped moisture leading to mold and mildew, and the easiest solution is to air dry. When you are finished with the washing machine, leave the door open until a swipe of your hand across the drum feels dry. When the dishwasher is finished, even if you have the dryer setting turned on, crack the door, lay a dish towel over the edge, and leave it slightly ajar until it dries inside. As for the garbage disposal, being wet is not the issue. Having trapped food is. Clear the chamber of all debris *(for the love of God stay away from the on switch)* and clean with the baking soda method. I like to use lemon juice instead of vinegar in this instance. And follow up with ice cubes with the disposal on to sharpen the blades. *Don't ask me how that works, but it does.* And while we are on the subject of appliances, clear the lint filter on the clothes dryer after you are finished using it.

- Change your furnace filters and clear your AC unit. Again, do this even if you are a renter. You can certainly ask your landlord (and you should) for the filters, because they can be pricey, but if you have a furnace unit in your place, this is a useful habit to get into that will make your furnace perform better and last longer. Change it every three months or when you switch from heat AC. As for the AC unit, if it is a big box unit outside, making sure it is clear of old leaves and any growth around it will keep it running in top shape. If you have a window AC unit, make sure to keep the filter dust and lint free by opening the front panel and vacuuming it out. You can also give it a quick wash in soap and water using a brush. Vacuum out the rest of the unit while you are at it. Do this at the start of the season and before you plug it in. *We want to be cool, not crispy.*

- As a writer, I sit at my desk for hours a day. Chairs with seat cushions will compress with repeated wear. That's just how foam works. You can use it until it's uncomfortable, or you can repair it by reupholstering and adding new padding. This task is not nearly as difficult as you'd think. Dining chair seats screw off from the base. Remove the fabric and foam, replace the foam, reapply the fabric, staple back into place, viola! If the entire chair is upholstered, that gets a bit more difficult but not impossible. You can certainly just add a purchased seat cushion to the chair seat and call it a day. Or, you could attempt to salvage the fabric so you can reapply it once you remove and replace the foam. Or, you could take this opportunity to replace the fabric on the seat with something new that coordinates once you've swapped out the foam. Do what works best for you. Especially if you love the chair in all other cases. Just keep in mind that we are fixing a problem, not creating another one by doing an upcycling project in a half-baked fashion. Make it nice! This is your home after all. You deserve it to be beautiful.

MAKE IT DO

There is very little that any of us actually need when it comes to our homes. Beyond the basics the rest is fluff, but it's the fluff that personalizes our space, so I understand completely wanting to add a bit extra. I've already discussed many ways to take something and make it more "you," but just for fun, let's do another project. One of my all-time favorite projects. One that I have done several times in my own home.

PROJECT: ALTERING ART
- any secondhand painted canvas (in a frame is even better)
- paints you have on hand (acrylic is easiest for cleanup, but if you have oils or even latex paint, it all works)
- various paint brushes and/or palette knives
- wash and rag for cleanup; vacuum for prep

You Don't Need It

This project has been met with a bit of debate. For some, the idea of taking someone else's artistic work and altering it is disrespectful. I say, original art in the back corner of a moldy antique store needs to be saved in any way it can. And if that means changing the color of the flowers to suit your home office, so be it.

1. Remove the painting from its frame (if it has one) and vacuum both the canvas and the frame very well to remove any dust. Paint doesn't like dust *and neither do I.*

2. Remove and discard all the old picture wire and hardware. Gently wash the frame to remove dust, oils, etc. Check it for damage and make repairs. Decide if you will paint it or leave it as is.

3. Re-staple the canvas backing if necessary.

4. Prepare your work area with paints, tools, and cleaning supplies.

5. Decide what will stay from the original painting and what you will alter. *I like to leave a large portion of the original work alone as an homage to the first painter. Covering the entire thing is up to you.*

"Use It Up, Wear It Out, Make It Do, or Do Without"

6. Start reimagining this upcycle and go for it! It's all yours now!

7. Repaint the frame if you are doing that, too.

8. Once the painting is to your liking and completely dry, reinstall it into the frame, use nails, staples, or heavy duty tape to hold it in place, and install new or newly cleaned hardware and picture wiring.

9. Hang proudly! *The satisfaction I have gained from these projects is immeasurable.*

TOTAL COST: FREE - $30

If you happen to find a free piece of art somewhere or from someone and you have paints and supplies on hand, this is a no-cost upcycle. If you have to buy the artwork or paints (or both), don't pay more than $20 for the artwork in a frame or $15 without a frame, depending on the size, and buy a few tubes of acrylic paint you can mix to create all the colors you want. And one more piece of advice: You are unlikely to discover a long-missing DaVinci painting at your local Goodwill, but it happens. Check into it if there is any question (though DaVinci probably didn't use canvases stamped with a Michael's Crafts label).

OR DO WITHOUT

Perspective time.

At the end of the day, you don't need much. Doing without is not a punishment. See how long you can hold out from buying something. Get creative with it. When you actually do buy, the satisfaction will be that much more exciting, like you've earned it with your patience and fortitude. I'd say fifty percent of the time, you will wind up never purchasing the item. You've gone this long without it, maybe you don't really want/need it after all. Think of the money you'll save by just saying "no…for the moment."

* * *

STORY TIME FROM BEFORE YOUR TIME

"Regrets, I've had a few. But then again, too few to mention" (a line from the famous song "My Way," popularized by Frank Sinatra). But yes, I do have one big regret in the *didn't-need-it, really-wanted-it, hesitated-and-then-it-was-gone* home decor genre.

The story I'm about to tell you is one of longing and missed opportunity, but it does not overshadow the fact that there have been a million little regretful purchases since then that I wish I had not made. Most of the time you will not go wrong by saying "no." If it's truly meant to be, it will be. Nine out of ten times.

I had moved from Hoboken, NJ to Morristown, NJ.

"Use It Up, Wear It Out, Make It Do, or Do Without"

I was taking a break from unpacking by browsing the furniture department at Bloomingdale's at the Short Hills Mall, never imagining I would find anything I could afford to buy and so I was safe from spending. But that's when I stumbled upon a piece so unique, so special, and so "not me," yet it drew me in. And it was on sale! Ready to hear what it was?

It was an overstuffed, purple velvet chaise lounge with turned cherrywood legs and gold upholstery nails around the seam. Lying on it was like lying on a supportive cloud, and I imagined myself spending long hours reading and napping. It was on sale, marked down from $1,800 to $600! Money that was hard to part with but something I was willing to consider for this piece of heaven. But purple? What was I thinking? I didn't own anything purple and probably never would. I would have to build everything around it, and that meant even more money I didn't have. But I wanted it! So bad!

I sat there contemplating for some time. Salespeople came and went offering help, but I just kept saying, "I'm still thinking." Finally, I left to meet a friend for dinner and discussed it with her. She was far better with money than I was, and she told me to wait until the following weekend. If it was still there, then put it on layaway instead of a credit card. *(For those born after 1990, layaway was a purchasing agreement where a store held an item for a customer after a deposit was made, allowing the customer to pay the remaining amount in installments over a set period, after which they could take the item home.)* Her reasons were many, none of which I need explain since layaway is no longer a thing. And in the end it didn't matter anyway, because a week later it was gone.

The moral of the story is, I still think about it, I would have made it work even in purple, and all I want to do right now is take a nap. But just so you know, regrets of this caliber rarely if ever happen. Do without!

8

Pretend You Have to Flee

I'm not sure what it is about natural disasters, cyberattacks, or zombie movies that I'm drawn to, but I have a feeling it has to do with the idea of taking just your most precious belongings, packing it all into every square inch of a car, and racing to safety. The idea of driving off-road in my Jeep is a bonus.

The California wildfires had me contemplating the urgency of an actual event. If I had just one hour's notice to evacuate my home, knowing there was a very real possibility everything else would be destroyed, what would I save? Talk about priorities!

But because of those events and many others we are living through, I've already written down my plan. OK, that's a lie. I didn't write it down; it's etched on my brain from anxiety-induced mental gymnastics in reaction to watching the news and scrolling social media. And it didn't *just* happen. It's been in my brain for decades. Planning calms me down. But enough about me. I know that one hour would be used in its entirety to collect my cranially-branded list of items from around the house, pack everything in the car, and lock down and secure my home in such a way that I had the best chance of coming back to it in one piece, depending on the disaster. *I think my crazy is showing.*

But in playing out this scenario, I unintentionally stumbled upon a new way to look at your belongings— **what would you take if you had one hour to gather and get out?** As you've seen before in this book, some of these ponderings have less to do with you as someone just starting out and more to do with the older generations, but they also serve as cautionary tales. **And in this case, always having an exit plan.** Things will happen in your life. Ones that require you put into perspective the very question: **what is absolutely necessary?** And for that you need to be prepared.

Not everything you own is precious. And even if it is, in an emergency situation compounded by limited time and space you'd have to ask yourself, is it essential? It's a tough call. Precious may be certain jewelry or photos. Essentials would be your phone, your laptop, your medication. Your pet turtle Shelly could be classified as both. But it can't all go with you, so some nonessentials will have to be left behind. In that case, my advice would be to do what you can to give them the best chance of survival. As terrifying as it would be to flee, you can at least rest easy in the knowledge that you have everything you will need in the short term and you've done all you can for everything else.

Can you even imagine someone who has a houseful of objects they "can't part with" being struck numb by the idea of choosing what to grab? Or having their things so scattered, they can't find the most important items in the limited time they have? I'm not talking about deciding which Matisse to pull off the wall. *(The answer is all of them; although, if you own even one Matisse I assume you have some kind of waterproof, fireproof, alarm system in place that would lock it down, but I digress.)* I'm talking about any number of people staring into their closet deciding what to pack. *(The answer is the clothes on your back and everything from your underwear/sock drawer.)*

* * *

Let's play a game. Yes, this will be a game that only somewhat aligns with the setting-up-your-first-home topic, but I believe as your pseudo mother in this case, it will be a lesson in safe housekeeping nonetheless.

The alert has gone out. There is a hurricane coming in the next 24 hours and you are in an evacuation zone. You, your roommate, and your dog have to be in your car and on the road to safety as quickly as possible. There is a good chance the longer you wait the more traffic there will be, so you need to act fast. You don't know what accommodations you will have once you get to where you are going, so you have to be prepared for all kinds of less-than-ideal situations. And why don't we add to the mix that you live in a second story apartment and the storm is predicted to be a Category 5 (that's 157 MPH or more), so there is a better-than-average chance your windows will shatter. Go!

Any ideas? 24 hours is a good amount of time, but remember, you are not the only ones leaving. And you are an apartment dweller, so it's doubtful you have plywood and sandbags just sitting around, *unless your landlord is uber prepared for these events.* What would you do? I know what I would do.

"Well then, tell us already, Bonnie!"

"Haha. OK."

Here's where having two of you is helpful to get double the work done.

PROJECT: "PACK IT UP AND MOVE IT OUT"

- **If you are both going to take your cars, then both of you need gas.** Hopefully, you have known about this storm for a few days, so you are filled up, but if not, one of you has to get gas in their car, then come back and do the same for the next car.

- While this is happening, the other roommate will be **moving any items from a downstairs garage or storage unit up to the apartment** to prevent these items from being flooded.

However, DO NOT waste time doing this if there is nothing important or the items can handle the water. Likewise, **any outdoor items like furniture, grills, and windchimes that can be dislodged and become projectiles in the wind should also be brought inside.**

- Begin packing the car that is still parked at home with all the essentials. **Food, water, medicine, first aid items, tools, blankets, towels, personal electronics and chargers/cords, personal identification and banking/insurance/legal paperwork (which should all be in a strong, water/fireproof box to begin with), flashlights, and certainly any rain gear, emergency gear, and safety gear.** *I leave that last one up to interpretation.* **And don't forget any pet-related items. Pack changes of utilitarian clothes;** *there won't be a fashion show going on in the shelter.*

- At this point, hopefully, both cars have been gassed up and you can both now work to prep the apartment for high winds and water damage. Like I said before, you probably won't have anything to board your windows with, so do what you can to minimize the possible damage. **Raise things off the floor. Unplug all items. Block windows from the inside if possible (which won't prevent them from**

> **breaking but may limit the cleanup), put breakables and wall decor away in cabinets and closets, and close all interior doors.**
>
> - **Walk the dog** and put them in one of the cars. Take a final look around the apartment to **see if you've done all you can and packed all you should. Make a plan** in case you get separated, unless you are heading to different locations.
>
> - **Lock up** and say a prayer, knowing you've done all you could to prepare, and the only thing that matters now is your physical safety. **Then get out of the storm's path!**

This same basic procedure can be modified for all scenarios. **If you have to shelter in place, presumably you had some forewarning so you can gas your cars, stock up on food and supplies, and charge all your electronics for when the power goes out,** all ahead of time. If you have just an hour's notice like those California wildfires, do the best you can, as quickly as possible, and get out. Zombie apocalypse? Move your vehicle close to your house in case you need to escape, barricade yourself inside blocking all doors and windows, stay in the center-most parts of the house, don't use anything that emits light, sound, or heat. Alien invasion? Hope they are friendly and just want to take you back to their home planet as a pet. If they treat you half as well as most of us treat our pets, that's a pretty good life.

So where does this leave us with regards to home organizing and interior design and setting up your first home? This was a lesson in preparedness. No matter where you live, natural disasters and major weather events can take place. Being prepared doesn't mean having a bunker of canned goods and ammunition and a bug out bag ready by the door 24/7. It just means being smart, being realistic, and being reasonable. Which is really what this whole book has been about. At the end of the day, choose the stuff in your home wisely, love it all, but always remember most of it is replaceable. You are not!

* * *

STORY TIME FROM BEFORE YOUR TIME

No story time. Readying yourself for a zombie apocalypse civil war was enough of a story. Besides, the aliens are probably going to want to dress you up in some stupid outfit like we do to our pets, so you won't need to pack all your clothes. Just something for the trip.

9

Don't Live in Lack

You've made it to the last chapter in the book! Great! Then it's time to discuss my final thoughts on your home and living in it by telling you one of my biggest pet peeves. That is when people look down their noses at secondhand items, whether clothes or cars or furnishings, because in their world view only new and shiny is acceptable. I cannot stress enough that new is not better. New, in many cases, is crap. *(There, I said it!)*

* * *

SIDE NOTE: This is a huge subject. And since I am not a mental health professional, the following is purely based on my observations as a home organizer for various clients, a public speaker on the subject, a consumer myself, and someone who has observed from the inside how marketing and retail have trained us over time. You may very well disagree with my take on this topic, but I hope you will use it to inform your own decisions and buying power.

* * *

I'm going to break this down into the who, why, where, what, when, and how of this subject as I see it. The following is an all-too-familiar American mindset. Many if not most of the clients I've worked with reached their current state of overwhelmedness in the same way—**over-consumption of low-cost, mass-produced goods, home furnishings, and "organizing solutions," bought with the intent of upscaling the appearance and function of their space.**

WHO

Generally speaking, those in this group occupy a lower-to-middle-class income lifestyle, though it does also apply to those who have moved into higher income brackets. They work and have some discretionary income, but may also carry a good deal of debt, and from time to time they may have life events that cause them to self-soothe by spending money on tangible things they can own. They have bought into the idea that something new and expensive proves their worth and value as people, they knowingly or unknowingly idolize the wealthy and the spending power they have, and as a result, they buy more to make themselves feel like they aren't "less than." However, the items purchased either overextend what they can afford or are cheaper versions of those aspirational items, so ultimately these products never quite give them the same satisfaction.

SIDE STORY: One such example comes to mind... the Walmart "fake" Birkin bag. Or what it has come to be affectionately called, a Firkin. Yes, it is leather. Yes, it resembles the iconic Hermes staple. And yes, at around $85 it's a whole lot less than $30K! But who are you trying to fool?! You got it at Walmart for Christ's sake! Or maybe you're not trying to fool anyone. Maybe you want them to know you're taking a stand against overpriced luxury brands. But I'll tell you what I'm looking at. Someone who paid nearly $100 for a knockoff. And an impractical one at that. Something that ultimately doesn't make you feel rich but does kinda make you look like you're trying too hard. And let's be serious for a moment. You don't actually love the Birkin bag, you love what it symbolizes—wealth. Which it doesn't if you get it from Walmart.

I have a better idea. Go to your local thrift store. Find a leather bag that meets your needs (size, color, style, strap length), then take it home and clean it up with some saddle soap and leather conditioner. Better yet! Go through the bags you already have and make one work for your needs now. Clean it up, maybe a quick repair or two, hook on a bangle for bling and call it a day. $0 spent. 100% useful and repurposed! Better all around for your wallet, the environment, and ultimately, your ego.

WHY

They spend to feel like they have more money than they do. Their self-worth is attached to feeling like a person with wealth and social status in a society that highly values those traits. They may feel insecurities held over from childhood about not having enviable items other kids had. They may feel that buying and owning things that those of a higher social status possess puts them in the same company. At the very least, they will have more than those in their own income bracket. Their lives are not built on "enough" but on "excess," and yet they still feel insignificant and unfulfilled. They lack the gratitude necessary to feel happy with what they have. Even when the buying takes on a generous tone such as gift giving, the number of items purchased always seems to hold more value to them than purchasing one item for the same amount of money. Cheaply made is preferred over higher quality, not just for the price point but for an unconscious need to repurchase the item in question when it no longer functions or is easily damaged. "More" in their minds is always better, but even that they struggle to reconcile with when their homes are overburdened

Don't Live in Lack

and uninviting. That's when the purchasing of storage items enters the picture as a way to contain all their possessions, so they still don't feel a need to stop themselves from acquiring more or downsizing what they have. They are, in essence, trying to buy happiness.

WHERE

These purchases take place mostly in big box stores like Target and Walmart, discount stores like T.J.Maxx, Marshalls and Homegoods (all under the same parent company), warehouse stores like Sam's Club (owned by Walmart) and Costco, off-season equivalents of parent department stores (like Nordstrom Rack or Saks Off Fifth), or online through Amazon. These locations offer low price points, multitudes of products to choose from, and immediate gratification of ownership, which is the driving force behind the "Buy Now" button on Amazon.

WHAT

Purchases are generally price-driven, allowing more items to be purchased in a single transaction. In store, well-lit and attractive displays and presentations offering products at a reasonable cost promote impulse shopping even when the item is not needed. The allure of efficiency and function and even the concept of minimalism pushes the required storage solutions to house the items bought.

WHEN

Boredom and sadness are equally likely to evoke the desire to shop unnecessarily. More so when gift giving and house decorating are involved, like at the holidays. Retailers know this and have cultivated a near Pavlovian response from consumers to buy items and gifts associated with each holiday on the calendar, whether religious or secular.

HOW

Unfortunately, credit cards account for most of the payments, and oddly they are a driving force for such purchases since they provide the illusion of having money to spend even when there isn't any. *Capital One Shopping Research gives the following statistics [updated on 12/3/2024]:*

- Cash is now used in only **12%** of in-store transactions in the United States.
- **81%** of shoppers prefer to pay with cards over cash.
- Shoppers spend up to **4x** as much when they pay with credit cards instead of cash.

- Consumers are **twice** as likely to use credit cards rather than cash for any given transaction.
- **63%** of nationwide retail sales dollars are from credit card transactions.

So "what's wrong with a little retail therapy?" Let me count the ways. The generations before you most definitely have leaned into the saying "the one who dies with the most toys, wins." *So many in fact, I have a job because of it.* But to truly understand where this all came from, we have to step back about 80 or so years to see what was happening in the US. I'm no historian but the broad strokes of it are:

1. World War II ends
2. Soldiers come home and start families
3. Affordable housing and suburban developments grow
4. Manufacturing in the US booms
5. Consumer goods are on the rise
6. Advertising pushes the "need" for new products and technology for the home
7. Credit cards come into existence
8. and with it all, the American Dream of the "white picket fence" and "keeping up with the Joneses" becomes a reality for many

You Don't Need It

But doesn't consumerism help the economy? Is credit card debt really that bad? So what if there is stuff stacked in every corner of my house? So what if I'm not using it? It's mine, I paid for it (or at least Citibank did), and I can live any way I want.

That's very true. But this has been going on for decades, and millions of people have been doing it. The cumulative effects are profound. And, it's not all about you. For every laminate covered, MDF (medium density fiberboard), home-assembled shelving unit purchased to support your growing assortment of things in multicolored baskets, you set off a chain of events that affect the environment, labor laws, the environment a couple more times, and your own mental health in the process. Here's how it works:

1. Higher end furniture retailers set the tone for the next trend in the industry.

2. Lower priced wholesalers commission copies of these items from China and other countries because of the low manufacturing costs. These costs are low based on several unsettling factors, including lack of environmental safeguards on the materials used and the waste produced, and distastefully low wages and work conditions for their employees.

3. The product is then shipped to the US by ship or plane, leaving a carbon footprint. Then again from the port of entry to the warehouse, then to the store, then to your home.

4. Depending on your skill level in assembling the piece, how heavy the items you add to it are, the conditions it is put under (humidity, damage by use, etc.,) and its usefulness in your home before you no longer need it or want it, you will likely only keep it for a period of time, NOT forever since it is not made to last forever.

5. We as a society have accepted this arrangement that these low-cost solutions have built-in obsolescence—the rationale being that if it didn't cost much then it "doesn't owe you a dime" when it comes to the end of its lifespan, after which you think nothing of putting it out with the trash. *Because in many cases, that's what it is.*

6. And what happens to trash? It gets carted off to a landfill, where it piles up with other non-biodegradable debris, leaching toxins into the water supply or gases into the air. If not here, then it's shipped abroad to wind up on a beach littering the natural beauty and killing off the wildlife.

So even though it may seem an easy, low cost fix to the problem of your stuff, you can see that it affects the entire world. Yes, the environment for sure, but also our humanity when we think about how little the people who manufacture these items make, and under what conditions. That doesn't even take into account the overwhelming stress on our bodies to be surrounded by stuff all the time. It's a basic Feng Shui principle that inorganic objects block positive energy—in other words, *the more plastic crap, the less overall wellbeing your home will provide.*

But this wasn't always the case. In the earlier part of the 20th century and before, furniture and home decor used to be better made. Items had names branded into them that meant quality, craftsmanship, enduring style, and longevity. They were items you used and loved, but took great care of by cleaning and repairing them. More importantly, they were items you saved money for before buying. There were no credit cards. The hope was that they would be passed down so future generations wouldn't have to buy their own. The quality would last.

But in the advent of those previously listed events after WWII, manufacturers soon learned they could make a bigger profit by making inferior products cheaper and faster, and therefore they boosted production. Marketing and advertising touted the "new," which with increased production came more frequently throughout the year. *What comes to mind is the creation of holiday furnishings that not only adorn your everyday decor but actually replace them. I have never had the desire to swap out my framed artwork for large scale portraits of Santa, but apparently other people do.* And, credit cards filled in the gaps in wages so no one had to save for "one day." They could own it now and not feel the pinch of spending cash in the process

This has all led us to today, when mass consumption, overspending, and increased clutter is a given in our everyday lives. But there is one last component of this lifestyle that doesn't get as big a spotlight, and that's the overwhelming feeling of lack. Let me explain with a story:

STORY (NOT ON THE SIDE): Since beginning my writing career I no longer work directly with clients, but in some cases I will offer advice remotely to people who request it. I received one such request from someone not quite local but in state, who, after reading my first book, asked if I would make an exception and organize their home. I declined but we did arrange to discuss the situation they found themselves in over Facetime.

With their iPad in hand, they walked me around what they deemed to be the two biggest problem areas in their house—the kitchen and the family room. Clutter was definitely an issue, as was buying in bulk without available space, and no visible systems in place to keep it in order. But it was during the discussion about what they hoped for and how they viewed what they had that the real problem became apparent. They weren't interested in changing their habits; they didn't think the way they were living was all that bad. "If only we had more room." "If only we had the budget to redo the kitchen." "If only the kids weren't such slobs." *Oh, the kids that learned their habits from you?*

They were wishing for more room so they didn't have to stop buying in bulk. They were wishing for a new kitchen so the dirty, disorganized one they had would just magically disappear. They blamed the kids because they couldn't blame themselves; that would be admitting that they created this mess. Now that we had walked and talked *(and I wasn't trying to secure a client so I could be bluntly honest)*, I asked them how they felt in their house.

"It's chaos."

"We have no room to do anything."

"He buys things again because he doesn't want to look for them."

"She keeps buying things that are supposed to make life easier, but they just take up space."

"The kids leave stuff everywhere."

"We can't have people over because there is nowhere to sit."

"His mother came over the other day." [She started to choke up when she said this.] "And she said to me, 'Oh God. It looks like an episode of "Hoarders" in here. How can you live like this?'"

That was when I told them I would review the

Don't Live in Lack

photos they gave me and get back to them in a few days with a plan they could implement on their own, in their own time. *I knew then that any work I did to give them instructions would go unheeded, but I enjoy a project and knew I'd use this story in a book one day.*

Looking again at the photos, I realized they didn't have any real furniture. The family room contained a well-worn rug that, with proper cleaning, would serve them well, but they hated it, saying it was left by the previous owners. There was an old couch that could not be used for seating because of the possibility of being stabbed with a spring—instead, it was a holding area for laundry baskets of unfolded clothes. The kids were sitting in Minecraft gaming chairs placed in front of the TV, which sat on a wood bench. And three fiberboard laminate cubbies *(like the ones I discussed earlier in this chapter)* lined the walls. The cubbies were filled with a variety of things: school books and papers, coats and sports equipment, old DVDs, dust-covered framed photos, junk mail, grocery bags, holiday decorations. *You get the picture.* One cubby was completely empty except for the multiple coffee cup rings warping the "wood." In the kitchen, there were no table and chairs. In their place were heavy duty wire shelving units filled with food, paper products, and bins of kitchen equipment. What didn't fit on the shelves was on the floor. The countertops were covered with small appliances and dishes (some clean, some not), leaving no open surfaces. Each cabinet was filled, but none with a specific category of item. It was a mess. And visibly dirty underneath.

Here's what I saw beneath what I could see. These were people that had been ignoring their home for some time. They had no systems. They had formed bad habits. They hated their place and their situation, and instead of dealing with it, they would shop, or in the kids' cases, play video games. They didn't have anything meaningful to them, so they treated it all poorly. I have a feeling a therapist would say this was a case of depression. I say, *having no training in the subject at all,* they needed to clean up their pigsty and show a little gratitude for the things they had, and then they'd feel better.

* * *

A few days later I emailed them and suggested the following:

DO NOT BUY ANYTHING, EITHER FOR THE PROJECT OR FOR YOUR DAY-TO-DAY, UNTIL YOU HAVE DOWNSIZED AND REORGANIZED WHAT YOU HAVE.

- Get rid of the couch. You don't have to replace it right now since you haven't had seating for some time.

- Take everything out of the cubbies and sort them into categories. Then put them where they belong. IF THE ITEMS DO NOT HAVE A HOME, THAT'S THE REASON THEY ARE FINDING THEIR WAY INTO THESE CUBBIES. Everything needs a home. Then clean the cubbies.

  → Outerwear does not fit in the coat closet? Install hooks at the door that everyone uses when they come into the house. Line shoes against the wall underneath. You could buy shoe trays, but you really don't need anything fancy for this. You probably already have something you can use, like old baking sheets, or cut the family room rug you dislike into foot wide strips to line the wall.

  → Add bins/baskets/containers to a column of cubbies for each child. Have them get involved in separating school work from sports equipment, gaming stuff from hobby stuff. Have them decide which container holds which items and tell them they are in charge of their own cubbies. And every week, they are responsible for cleaning through them and reorganizing. This will build the habit.

  → Do the same for the rest, either putting it back where it belongs or creating a permanent space for it in the cubbies. *Get rid of stuff too—it doesn't all have to go back.*

→ I suspect the empty cubby with the coffee rings is part of someone's morning routine. If that's the case, commit to it by putting a coaster there. Add a small dish for keys, wallet, etc. This is a chance for each of you to build new habits that will keep it all in shape.

→ Don't forget to continue to downsize as you go so you don't store things you have no use for.

→ Clean the room top to bottom, from windows and walls to rugs and floors. Then, imagine your ideal way of living in this space. Are you all watching TV together? Are you reading in the corner while the kids are doing homework? Is it a home gym? Whatever your vision, build the room around what you want/need, NOT what it's supposed to be. It's your house. Make it fit your needs.

→ Reset it before bed each night. No mess on the floor of things not put back to the right place. No laundry baskets of unfolded clothes lining the new couch. No mug of cold coffee sitting in its cubby. The more you neglect it, the easier the backslide into old habits. BUT the better you take care of it, the more you'll want to keep it neat. And it's not all on one person to do this.

You are a family, so everyone is responsible for treating the things in the house with respect, care, and gratitude.

→ Lastly, make it a weekly or at least monthly task to clean and reset it. **The more you do it, the less you'll have to do.**

Now, onto the kitchen.

- Gather all your paper supplies. Clear off as many shelves of one metal shelving unit as you need—ideally top shelves so nothing heavy ever falls on you. Clean them. Stack paper supplies. Do not buy until you have nearly depleted what you have.

- Gather all your non-perishable foods. Clear off as many shelves as needed—ideally center, eye-level shelves for easy access. Clean them. Check expiration dates; dispose of anything expired. Put like items together. Line up and stack in formation, largest in back. Any small items should be placed in a lidded container. SIDE PROJECT: Create a list of recipe ideas to use the items nearing expiration.

- Gather all your storage containers. Pair lids with bottoms. Recycle or dispose of anything discolored or melting from the microwave. Place them all in one large lidded bin and place on a bottom shelf. This way they stay contained.

- Gather all your small appliances. Again, clear off as many shelves as needed. Ideally, use lower shelves since the weight will help support the shelving unit. Any appliances that do not work can be disposed of. Any appliances that are missing vital pieces and therefore have not been used can be donated. Any appliances you are not using can be sold. Place appliances on shelves, with those you use most often in the front for easy access. Go through the same procedures for the appliances on the counter. You will now be building a habit of intentionally using them and putting them back when not in use so they are not always taking up surface area.

- Go through each drawer/cabinet, emptying it, washing it, separating/sorting the items inside, and downsizing what you do not use. Assign categories for each drawer/cabinet and put back what belongs. Do not put everything back. Do not keep anything broken or damaged. If you find an item along the way that belongs in a completely different space, put it back in its home.

- Depending on your supply of food items, you may consider using the cabinets for food and the shelves for surplus or bulk items.

- Create workstations on your kitchen counters, like a coffee bar, easy access kids' plates and cups,

Don't Live in Lack

cutting boards near the knives, etc. Whatever makes the most sense for how you live.

- Don't go to bed without at least putting dirty dishes in the dishwasher, even if you don't run it. Waking up to a sinkful of dirty dishes is no way to start your day.

- Keep a shopping list nearby to mark down what items you are running low on (truly low) or meal ingredients, and shop with the list. This will cut down on impulse buys and bulk buys, and keep your budget in check.

- If there are items you have not used in a year's time, make a point of using them, or donate them.

- Continue to check foods for expiration dates. If an item is reaching a date and you do not plan to use it, donate it to a local food pantry.

- If you cook regularly, the kitchen needs to be cleaned regularly. Weekly is best, when you can really tackle the job.

- Build habits with everyone in the family. Instead of leaving dishes on the counter or the table, make sure to stack them in the sink or dishwasher. If someone uses the last of something, it should be written on the shopping list. If a plate is chipped or cracked it is no longer food safe. Dispose of it or repurpose it—*perhaps a dish under a potted plant to collect water and dirt.*

But the most important task in all of this is to find and reclaim your things. Treat them well. Used them well. Build traditions around them. Find a favorite. Make it a family affair—the cleaning as well as the living. Value your belongings by taking care of them. And if you are not interested in doing that, then you don't need those things. They are just taking up room. Room that you told me was the number one thing you were looking for. If this all works, your home will have less chaos, everything will belong somewhere, you will save money by not buying things you already own, and your family will be involved in keeping the home neat so they feel invested in it as well. Try it out. Keep me posted on your progress. And Good Luck!

I'd like to say I heard back from them a month or so later with photos of clutter free spaces and happy faces, but I never heard from them again. And I know exactly why.

1. I wasn't doing the work for them and they didn't want to do the work.
2. It's easier to not fix the problem—that way you get to complain about it.

3. Complaining feels like power over your situation when power is what you feel is lacking from your life.

* * *

I don't want you to live like that. I don't want anyone to live like that. Feeling powerless in your life, feeling like you'll never "get there," always looking at the glass half empty. That sense of lack, of being less than. It's a way of treating your things like they are not worthy of the lifestyle you deem good enough.

The quickest way I know to flip that switch is gratitude for all you have. Stop wasting money. Start taking care of the things you have. Build healthy habits about your belongings. Cultivate traditions with your family around respect for your surroundings. Don't take what you have for granted. You don't need more stuff, more space, more time. You need to be thankful for everything you already have and treat it lovingly. Once you do that, your attitude towards your life takes on a whole new view. *Probably because there won't be any clutter blocking it.*

* * *

You Don't Need It

STORY TIME FROM BEFORE YOUR TIME

I used to know envy. Envy used to make me wish I had other people's lives. Envy would make me want more stuff so I'd look and feel successful to those people whose lives I wished I had. Envy had a way of telling me, "you aren't anyone unless you are looking up at someone ahead of you on the ladder and working to be more like them." I wish I had long ago told envy to go F* themselves.

But age has a way of maturing (if you're lucky) your view on certain things, and while I still know envy, we don't interact nearly as much as we did. In fact, envy changed its name to "appreciate." I appreciate the traits or talents of others, so I'd rather learn from them than be them. I appreciate that I now know success comes from living well and enjoying your life. And when I appreciate others and all that I have, I'm grateful for both. As long as I'm happy and healthy and have people who love me in my life, there is not a whole lot more that I need.

Is my life perfect? No. But I get up every morning and I'm filled with gratitude—for what I have and who is in my life, for the talents I possess and the personality traits that make me me, for the life I'm building and the dreams I'm making into reality. And not one of those things can be bought.

This is the life I want for you. In my case, it was a hard fought battle that made me stronger for having gone through it, but boy do I wish I had gotten here sooner. Take this as your cautionary tale—get to this place in fewer years, so you'll have more life ahead to enjoy it.

Final Advice

How do we get off this hamster wheel and live our best lives? *I'm so glad you asked.*

I've talked a lot about being intentional with your purchases. In my ideal world, when it comes to the things we put in our homes, with the exception of appliances and electronics, which I will admit need to be new, **I would love to see a drastic decline in the manufacturing of fast furnishings. Unfortunately, that will only ever happen if consumers stop consuming.** There are more than enough tables, chairs, dressers, fine china, coffee mugs, and all manner of tchotchkes in the world already. Whatever you need or want is already made. If it's not sitting in your great uncle's storage unit he's been paying rent on since the 80s, it's most definitely at your local thrift, vintage, secondhand, or antique store. Or the next yard sale. Or being given away from free on the side of the road. But I promise you, it's out there. And with a bit of creativity, you can make anything that is not exactly what you wanted be exactly what you want. For pennies on the dollar. By salvaging something from a landfill. Without creating an environmental nightmare. And it's probably made so well it will last through all your decorating mood swings.

I've also talked about the difference between needs and wants, and how consumerism has trained us to "need" certain items, even if you have never used and probably will continue to not use them for the rest of your life. **Only ever fill your lives with things, people, and experiences that serve a need or feed your soul.** Everything else is just extra, and extra turns into way too much, way too fast.

I've talked about maintaining your surroundings so they are functional for your lifestyle, as well as a reflection of your tastes, personality, and priorities. Your home should never become a burden or a responsibility, or just a place to eat, shower, and sleep. Plan your home around *your* wants and needs and no one else's (with the exception of the people you live with.) It should function for the way you live, not the way you're "supposed" to live. But remember, a functioning home is an organized home. Make a plan, build habits to maintain it, reassess when it's not working. And keep it clean. A clean home is one where you respect your life and yourself.

And I've talked about staying away from the mindset of "my stuff is garbage so why take care of it?" I've been in enough houses that have looked like a dumpster behind a Walmart during a garbage strike to know that living with that attitude will only make things worse over time. Respect yourself enough to care about how you live while also living within your means.

YOU DESERVE TO LIVE YOUR BEST LIFE, ALWAYS! Neither money nor job title should stop you from having a home that fills you with positive energy, comfort, and bliss. If your home isn't the place you want to run to when the outside world has been less than kind, make a change. That's your home's only purpose—to provide shelter from the storm of everything going on in the world. All the "essentials" and "must haves" and "new and improved" won't bring you to that place. What will? Just enough, just what you love, infused with a bit of you. Otherwise, **YOU DON'T NEED IT!**

A Note To Booksellers:

YOU DON'T NEED IT is the third in a series about efficient living, and is specifically focused on setting up your first home in a way that will require less lifetime organizing and cleaning, with tips on lifestyle systems and practical decor. My first book, *STOP BUYING BINS,* focused on downsizing to get the reader to the point where they could apply the subject covered in my second book, *STOP PUSHING PERFECTION*—i.e., organizing what was left. In my role as a professional home organizer and interior decorator, I repeatedly found that creating workable spaces and streamlined living areas, building routines to manage those spaces efficiently, and applying practical decor principles were paramount to both a beautiful and functional home. What better way to start out in the world on your own!

I would be so grateful if you would carry my books in your store. And I hope you enjoy reading them as much as I enjoyed writing them. Thank you for your consideration.

www.ingramcontent.com/pod-product-compliance
Lightning Source LLC
Chambersburg PA
CBHW072000070526
44583CB00015B/1275